Marriage Records
of
Barbour County, Alabama
- 1838-1859 -

Compiled by:
Helen S. Foley

Southern Historical Press, Inc.
Greenville, South Carolina

SOUTHERN HISTORICAL PRESS, INC.
PO BOX 1267
Greenville, SC   29601

ISBN #978-0-89308-657-6

Printed in the United States of America

FORWORD

The names in this volume were copied as they appeared in the marriage book and were checked for accuracy with the 1850 Census of Barbour County, Alabama, by Mrs. S. E. Godfrey, genealogist of the county. However, all names are not in the census, but were corrected from her experience in working with the courthouse records as follows:

Artimitis	=	Artemsia	Gerkey	=	Gerke
Avent	=	Avant	Giss	=	Gist
Boilston	=	Boyleston	Hearin	=	Hearn
Brizzell	=	Brizzell	Homes	=	Holmes
Buckhats	=	Buckhalter	Hollen	=	Holland
Canada			Jerimeah	=	Jeremiah
Canady	=	Kennedy	Kitcham	=	Ketchum
Candry	=	Condry	Ledora	=	Leonidas
Carr, Trgan	=	Carr, Tryon	Louisetin	=	Lucretia
Cenada			Maldonta	=	Maldonetta
Cearcy	=	Searcy	Masedonia	=	Amanda
Chinchleen	=	Kinchen	Percelo	=	Priscilla
Christna	=	Christian	Pinkleton	=	Pinkerton
Curney	=	Kerney	Rasbury	=	Rasberry
Clemen	=	Clements	Right	=	Wright
Croppe	=	Craps	Retherford	=	Rutherford
Curinton	=	Curenton	Sanpta	=	Serepta
Curney	=	Kerney	Shelomath	=	Shelinith
Desazo	=	Deshazo	Tergwell	=	Turquill
Dicken	=	Dickson	Tilverton	=	Yelverton
Epthpsey	=	Epsey	Tompson, Huey B.	=	Tompson, Henry B.
Faknard	=	Farquhar	Volentine	=	Valentine
Foutch	=	Fouch	Willice	=	Willis
Fuqua, Randall	=	Fuqua, Randolph			
Gann	=	Gunn			

MINISTERS PERFORMING MARRIAGES

Andrews, A. S.
Andrews, Mark S.
Armstrong, Saul
Barker, G. W.
Bass, Augustus C.
Bass, James
Belcher, Abner
Belcher, Phillip
Brooks, Middleton
Brooks, R. B.
Brown, Reubin E.
Buys, James
Cadenhead, James
Calloway, P. M.
Capers, Stephen D.
Carter, G. W.
Carter, John C.
Clement, J. A.
Cody, Edward
Collins, James L.
Collins, John D.
Cowan, John G.
Crowell, John
Cumbie, Andrew
Cumbie, Daniel
Cumbie, J. J.
Curry, Cary
Cushman, George
Cushman, George S.
Daniel, James L.
Danner, J.
Davis, Jonathan
Davis, W. M.
Dawson, J. E.
Dickson, J. J.
Douglas, D. S. T.
Eldridge, Peter
Ellis, William J.
Ellison, William H.
Evans, Charles
Fleming, Oliver

Gallaway, William
Gay, J. L.
Glenn, J. W.
Glenn, T. W.
Glenn, Thompson
Golson, L. P.
Grace, Francis T.
Graham, J. N.
Griffin, James
Griffith, James
Groves, John J.
Guice, Thomas
Harrison, L. C.
Harrod, James
Haygood, Appleton
Hearn, P. C.
Helms, Aaron
Holston, J. W.
Hunt, C. S.
Hunter, John
James, Edwin
Jordan, J. W.
Jordan, Junius
Keith, Robert
Lee, William
Loveless, B. D.
Luker, William
Malone, Green
Mathews, M.
McCarty, W. A.
McNeely, O. D.
McIntosh, Wm. H.
McMillan, Anonee
McNair, Evander
Miller, William P.
Moss, F. H.
Motley, William M.
Neal, William B.
Neily, O. D.
Nix, Zacheous
Norton, W. K.

Oliver, John L.
Oliver, Mathew
Owens, James N.
Padgett, Moses
Parker, C. A.
Patterson, A. M.
Patterson, J. W.
Payne, William
Pelham, C. S.
Pelham, Uriah M.
Pelham, Uriah W.
Perry, Dow
Phillips, S. A.
Pilly, S. A.
Pilly, Stephen F.
Powell, G. W.
Purnell, G. W.
Robinson, W. C.
Ross, William
Scales, Nicholas P.
Sealy, Thomas H. D.
Seller, H. L.
Shanks, J.

Shores, James W.
Sikes, Solomon
Sims, Joel
Smith, R. C.
Sterns, H.
Sterry, Harris
Talley, G. R.
Thigpen, Joseph
Tiller, H. L.
Tison, James G.
Toler, Robert
Tomlin, Jesse
Tyson, Jonathan G.
Walkey, T. C. V.
Ware, Edward R.
Warnick, John
Weston, W. W. B.
Wilks, W.
Williams, Elisha
Winn, P. C.
Worthy, A. N.
Van Hoose, A.
Van Hoose, E. Y.

JUSTICES OF THE PEACE PERFORMING MARRIAGES

Adkinson, W. N.
Aplin, Joseph
Atkinson, W. N.
Avent, M.
Baker, Alpheus, Jr.
Baker, Franklin E.
Barron, B. A.
Baxter, James S.
Bethune, William M.
Beverly, B. F.
Blakey, A.
Blanchet, Henry
Bludworth, Peyton
Bludworth, Thomas F.
Britt, Ira
Brown, B. A.

Brown, R. E.
Bush, Council
Bush, D. A.
Campbell, Daniel
Cargile, Thomas
Clark, James
Cobb, A. M.
Cole, J. S.
Cole, J. T.
Cox, John
Crews, William B.
Croppe, Benjamin
Danforth, J. H.
Daniel, Joseph
Daniel, Z. J.
Dent, S. H.

Efurd, G. C.

Efurd, T. C.

Faulk, Henry, Jr.

Flake, Seborn J.

Ford, Eli N.

Fraser, Malcom

Gary, James

Gilchrist, M.

Gilchrist, Malcom

Gillis, Donald

Hall, Mathew

Hardman, Jack

Head, William

Helms, John

Hightower, Thomas A.

Hinson, William

Holland, Jesse

Hood, J. T.

Johnston, James B.

Jones, A. E.

Jones, J. A.

Jones, J. P.

Jones, William K.

Jones, William R.

Fosey, J. J.

Justice, A. H.

Kiezer, B. H.

Lewis, Oats S.

Lightner, S. F.

Lightner, Samuel S.

Lochala, Thomas

Lowe, R. N.

Mann, William B.

Martin, D. A.

Mathison, Malcom

McCormick, William

McEachern, Gilbert

McGilvary, Duncan

McInnis, Miles

McKenzie, D.

McLendon, J. G.

McMurray, G. J.

McMurray, William M.

McNab, D.

McNair, John P.

Miles, William A.

Moreland, H. H.

Nobles, Archibald

Oppert, H.

Orr, James

Payne, A. E.

Pearson, B. F.

Pierce, Lovard L.

Pipkin, H.

Pipkin, Haywood

Purswell, Gabriel

Quattlebum, John

Ray, Elijah

Reaves, H. F.

Reid, John

Richards, T. W.

Riley, Joseph

Rist, Amos

Roberts, S. B.

Russell, H. C.

Sanders, W. P.

Scales, C. S.

Scarborough, James A.

Scroggins, G. R.

Sellers, Benjamin D.

Shanks, James

Shaw, William M.

Shora, S. K.

Sims, W. R.

Sinquefield, Asa

Smith, William

Smith, Williamson

Snead, William M.

Spence, A. T.

Stephen, William G.

Stephens, Oats

Stephens, William J.

Stewart, J. R.

Stewart, Peter

Stokes, Silas A.
Thomas, D. K.
Thornton, J. M.
Tompkins, H. M.
Van Epps, A. C.
Vinson, Wesley
Warr, E. S.
Wellborn, M. B.
Wellborn, W. B.
Weston, D. M.
White, John H.
White, J. M.

Wiley, W. A.
Williams, Buckner
Williams, D. D.
Williams, G. W.
Williams, George W.
Williams, John L.
Williams, John N.
Williams, Wilson G.
Wilks, E. M.
Wood, Young
Wood, Z.

OTHERS PERFORMING MARRIAGES

Banks, B. H.
Banks, B. T. G.
Brown, J. R. W.
Clayton, Isaac, Elder
Corbitt, J. W., S. D.
Cowen, Wm. R., Judge
Crymes, Thomas P.
Flowers, Wright
Foster, Thomas H.
Glenn, J. E.
Glenn, L. S.
Glenn, Thompson
Grantham, A.
Greathouse, R. M.
Harris, J. J.
Heard, James A.
Lee, William, Elder
Mallard, James H.

McDonald, Walter H.
McIntosh, John R.
McIntosh, William H.
Mathews, James
Nichols, Joel
Norton, John
Norton, J. W.
Scales, N. D.
Shanks, William T.
Shorter, Jno. Gill, Judge
Story, James
Ward, Edward R.
Ware, E. R.
Weaver, J. C.
Williams, J. S., Judge

Elijah Anders and Lucinda Byrd, issued 6 Aug. 1838, return not
        recorded. Page 2.

Reden Bullard and Clarisa Glass, issued 2 Oct. 1840, return not
        recorded. Page 2.

Elvin Wainwright and Charlotte Oliver, 23 Dec. 1838, by Joseph
        Daniel, J. P. Page 2.

Ottis Edgington Farmer and Martha Volentine, issued 25 July 1841,
        return not recorded. Page 5.

John Cappleman and Willmouth Elder, issued 26 July 1841, return
        not recorded. Page 5.

Seth W. Boughton and Mary Jane Smith, issued 25 Sept. 1841,
        return not recorded. Page 5.

John F. Keener and Martha A. J. Hackney, 18 Nov. 1841, by Wm.
        McMurray. Page 5.

Josiah M. Carr and Martha Faison, issued 16 Dec. 1841, return
        not recorded. Page 6.

Arthur Lott and Bedsey McGaines, issued 7 Jan. 1842, return not
        recorded. Page 6.

Robert N. Jackson and Larella Mary Glenn, issued 16 Dec. 1842,
        return not recorded. Page 7.

Hardy Stephens and Sarah Reaves, 7 Jan. 1842, by Joseph Daniel,
        J.P. Page 12.

James M. Statun and Sally Bigford, 13 Jan. 1842, by Wm. McMurray,
        J.P. Page 12.

William Medly and Ellen Cook, 20 Jan. 1842, by Wm. M. McMurray,
        J.P. Page 13.

Daniel Swain and Lucinda Commander, 4 Nov. 1841, by Wm. B. Crews.
        Page 13.

Moses Daniel and Martha Ann Louise Williams, 13 May 1841, by
        W. C. Robinson, M.G. Page 14.

James G. Tison and Adrianna Ott, 12 Sept. 1841, by J. W. Norton.
        Page 14.

Archd. C. Stewart and Martha Ann Bass, 26 Aug. 1841, by John P.
        McNair, J. P. Page 15.

Hamilton Rachels and Sarah McNeal, 9 Apr. 1841, by W. B. Crews.
        Page 15.

Edward M. Heron and Mary McNeill, 4 Nov. 1841, by Joel Sims, M.G.
        Page 16.

Stephen Hines and Mary Hearn, 5 Dec. 1841, by Henry Faulk, Jr.,
        J.P. Page 16.

William W. Stephens and Martha Stafford, 1 Dec. 1841, by Wm. M.
        McMurray, J.P. Page 17.

1

John Gillis and Christian McIntosh, 18 Nov. 1841, by Joseph
    Daniel, J.P.   Page 17.

William B. Moore and Nancy Ann Smith, 15 Dec. 1841, by A. C.
    Van Epps, J.P.   Page 18.

Jeremiah Baugh and Martha Draper, 19 Dec. 1841, by W. B. Crews,
    J.P.   Page 18.

Jehue Raly and Seney Collins, 9 Dec. 1841, by John P. McNair,
    J.P.   Page 19.

Seaborn Lewis and Susan Wheeler, 2 Nov. 1841, by Buckner
    Williams, J.P.   Page 19.

Isham C. Browder and Mary Ann Martha Hilsman Tarver, 14 Sept.
    1841, by Joseph Daniel, J.P.   Consent of her
    father, B. H. Tarver, p. 171.   Page 20.

Abner H. King and Elizabeth Lewis, 4 Nov. 1841, by Wm. M.
    McMurray, J.P.   Page 20.

Duncan C. McCollum and Rosanah McRae, 28 Oct. 1841, by Wm. Shaw,
    J.P.   Page 21.

Elija J. Keahey and Sarah Smyley, 30 Sept. 1841, by A. Blakey.,
    Esq.   Page 21.

Thomas McMan and Margaret McRae, issued 20 Sept. 1841, executed,
    Wm. Shaw, J.P.   Page 22.

Thomas C. Kendrick and Martha Ann Feagan, 23 Sept. 1841, by
    Wm. A. McMurray, J.P.   Page 22.

Joel D. Stokes and Elizabeth Bush, 15 July 1841, by Z. Wood, J.P.
    Page 23.

James McGilvary and Sarah Jane Thomas, 8 Apr. 1841, by Wm. B.
    Mann, J.P.   Page 23.

William Baxley and Kitey Eliza Carrol, 10 June 1841, by John P.
    McNair, J.P.   Page 24.

William Sapp and Elizabeth Jones, 29 July 1841, by Buckner
    Williams, J.P.   Page 24.

Zabin Turner and Sarah Ann Cousins, 22 Sept. 1841, by Wm. M.
    Bethune, J.P.   Page 25.

Henry J. Hutto and Lydia Louise Sheperd, 1 Apr. 1841, by T. C.
    Efurd, J.P.   Page 25.

Warren Martin and Adah Ann Sellers, 26 Sept. 1841, by Wm. M.
    McMurray, J.P.   Page 26.

C. J. S. Kelly and Elizabeth Atwell, 25 Apr. 1841, by Z. Wood,
    J.P.   Page 26.

Wiley Hartzog and Espey Lee, 2 Sept. 1841, by William T. Shanks.
    Page 27.

John J. Norton and Nancy J. Floid, 29 July 1841, by A. Blakey,
    J.P.   Page 27.

Charles G. Brantly and Elvira Adams, 12 Sept. 1841, by A.
Blakey, J.P. Page 28.

James Jackson Ware and Nancy Matilda Chapman, 11 Nov. 1841, by
Jno. P. McNair, J.P. Page 28.

Wiley L. Taylor and Elizabeth Horn, 23 May 1841, by John A.
Williams, J.P. Page 29.

H. S. Hill and Elender Sorrell, 1 Sept. 1841, by Wm. M. McMurray,
J.P. Page 29.

Vemtine Earnest and Rachael Burns, 1 Feb. 1842, by Wm. Shaw, J.P.
Page 30.

Philemon H. Youngblood and Martha Keener, 30 Dec. 1841, by
James Clark, J.P. Page 30.

Christian Thomas and Joice Eliza Shepperd, 23 Dec. 1841, by
Joel Sims, M.G. Page 31.

Joseph Singleton and Mary Ann Williams, 28 Nov. 1841, by
Buckner Williams, J.P. Page 31.

Hosea Sellers and Eletha Thigpen, 18 Nov. 1841, by Wm. M.
McMurry, J.P. Page 32.

Vincent Carr and Louisa Cook, 18 Dec. 1841, by Wm. M. McMurry,
J.P. Page 32.

Murdock Gillis and Mary Booey, 13 Apr. 1841, by Wm. M. McMurry,
J.P. Page 33.

John O. C. Wilkinson and Ann Nevals, issued 6 Nov. 1840,
executed, W. M. Shaw, J.P. Page 33.

John Savage and Mary Dowling, 28 Feb. 1841, by Joseph Daniel,
J.P. Page 34.

Joseph Musgrove and Julian Jackson, 14 Mar. 1841, by James
Clark, J.P.

Allen Youngblood and Lurany Jane Semore, 1 Oct. 1840, by Malcom
Fraser, J.P.

Hartwell Ball and Jincy McCall, issued 3 Oct. 1840, executed,
W. M. Shaw, J.P.

Alexander McLeod and Catherine McIntosh, 20 June 1841, by Wm.
Head, J.P.

Daniel McLeod and Nancy Smith, 10 Apr. 1841, by D. K. Thomas,
J.P.

William Cowart and Susan W. Worthington, 26 Dec. 1841, by D. K.
Thomas, J.P.

Jefferson Smith and Susan Bush, 4 Feb. 1841, by J. L. Williams,
J.P.

Samuel Brown and Elizabeth Tilly, 5 Oct. 1840, by Joseph Daniel,
J.P. Consent of his guardian, William Tilly.

James Ford and Martha Sawyears, issued 21 Dec. 1840, executed, Wm. M. McMurry, J.P.

Tilman S. White and Susan Coleman, 8 Nov. 1840, by Joel Sims, M.G.

William R. Arrington and Seney Dikes, 21 Mar. 1841, by T. C. Efurd, J.P.

Elisha Worrel and Mary McMillon, 21 Jan. 1841, by Wm. B. Mann, J.P.

H. W. Wicker and Nancy Dowling, 25 Jan. 1841, by Wm. B. Mann, J.P.

John McGuire and Temperance Harrison, 18 Mar. 1842, by Wm. McCormick, J.P.

Washington Blackman and Margarett Ann Nichols, 20 Mar. 1842, by Wm. M. Bethune, J.P.

Monro Crocker and Eliza Lewis, 22 July 1841, by Wm. McCormick, J.P.

John Smith and Lisha Jane Cousins, 9 Apr. 1842, by Wm. M. Bethune, J.P.

William B. Saunders and Eliza J. Williams, 15 Feb. 1842, by John W. Norton.

Jerrod J. Spear and Mary Creach, 13 Mar. 1842, by Wm. Head, J.P.

Archibald Bigford and Emeline Hicks, 20 Jan. 1841, by T. C. Efurd, J.P.   Page 45.

Neal McDonald and Mary A. R. Harrison, 17 Feb. 1842, by Wm. McMurry, J.P.   Page 45.

David Smith and Jane Baker, 12 Jan. 1842, by Solomon Sikes, M.G. Page 46.

David Simmons and Rachael Davis, 18 Jan. 1842, by B. Williams, J.P.   Page 46.

William M. Bryan and Epthpsey Head, issued 30 Nov. 1841, return not recorded.   Page 47.

Thomas Cain and Lorany Holly, 9 Nov. 1841, by D. K. Thomas, J.P. Page 47.

Sandford G. Green and Rebecca Gaught, issued 12 Dec. 1840, return not recorded.   Page 48.

Harrel F. Reaves and Martha Bush, 28 Jan. 1841, by Wm. B. Mann, J.P.   Page 48.

James C. Roach and Clarrisy Patterson, 24 Feb. 1842, by Wm. B. Mann, J.P.   Page 49.

George W. Williams and Sarah A. Ryans, 15 Dec. 1841, by W. B. Mann, J.P.   Page 49.

Eli Thomas and Retincey E. Bush, 31 Dec. 1840, by Jno. L.

Williams, J.P.   Page 50.

George Bryan and Mary M. Head, 28 Oct. 1841, by D. K. Thomas, J.P.   Page 50.

Jackson Holland and Mary Ann Elizabeth Wimberly, 22 June 1841, by W. B. Crews, J.P.   Page 51.

John Stricklin and Rebecca Ayres, 2 Dec. 1840, by Z. Wood, J.P. Page 51.

David Dikes and Harriet McKinzie, 7 Dec. 1840, by W. N. Adkinson, J.P.   Page 52.

Redin Rutland and Clarisa Glass, 4 Oct. 1840, by Peter Eldridge, M.G.   Page 52.

Airial Jones and Matilda Baker, 17 Jan. 1841, by Joel Sims, M.G. Page 53.

William H. F. Harper and Elizabeth Ann Richardson, issued 25 Dec. 1840, executed, T. C. Efurd.   Page 53.

John C. McNeill and Mary A. Hamilton, 10 Mar. 1841, by Joel Sims, M. G.   Page 54.

Elisha U. Wilks and Susanah Hearn, issued 10 Nov. 1840, executed, W. M. Shaw, J.P.   Page 54.

Alexander Shipman and Mary Westbrook, issued 23 Jan. 1841, executed, Jno. H. White, J.P.   Page 55.

Reuben J. Cooper and Rebecca Austin, issued 18 Nov. 1840, executed, W. M. Shaw, J.P.   Page 55.

Joshua Mabury and Elizabeth Amanda Ziterower, issued 27 Nov. 1840, executed, W. M. Shaw, J.P.   Page 56.

John McLeod and Jane Cunningham, 26 May 1842, by Wm. B. Crews, J.P.   Page 56.

John Thomas and Christian Stewart, 17 Apr. 1842, by Wm. B. Crews, J.P.   Page 57.

Charles J. Branch and Nancy Herring, 8 May 1842, by A. Blakey, Esq.   Page 57.

James Holland and Mary Jane Simms, 17 Feb. 1842, by W. B. Crews, J.P.   Page 58.

Simeon Nichols and Mary Elizabeth Simmons, 22 Apr. 1842, by James Clark, J.P.   Page 58.

Roderick McNeill and Flora H. Cunningham, 7 Apr. 1842, by Wm. B. Crews, J.P.   Page 59.

Willis Smith and Miss F. Morrison, 11 May 1842, by Z. Wood, J.P. Page 59.

William R. Bush and Eliza Jones, 20 Dec. 1840, by J. L. Williams, J.P.   Page 60.

James Peeler made Deacon of the M. E. Church by Bishop James O.

5

Andrews, Montgomery, Ala., on 1 Jan. 1843. Recorded 12 Jan. 1843. Page 60.

James W. Holeston made Deacon in the M. E. Church on 20 Dec. 1835 at Tuskalossa, Ala., J. Soule. Page 61.

George W. Purnell made Elder in the M. E. Church on 8 Jan. 1832. Done at Augusta, Ga. Elijah Hedding. Page 62.

Joseph Cox and Letty Powell, 25 Oct. 1842, by D. Campbell, J.P. Page 62.

Aaron Helms, a Baptist preacher of Bethel Church, ordained, 18 Aug. 1843. William Payne, V.D.M. & M. W. Helms, V.D.M. Page 63.

David C. Lee and Kiziah Saunders, 10 Dec. 1843, by Zacheous Nix, M.G. Page 63.

John Sauls and Eliza Beckworth, 10 Oct. 1843, by Daniel Campbell, J.P. Page 64.

James E. Glenn and Jane E. Greer, 30 Jan. 1844, by John J. Groves, M.G. Page 64.

James B. Bishop and Nancy Streeter, 16 Feb. 1843, by Wm. M. Bethune, J.P. Page 65.

David Reaves and Mahala Evans, 13 Nov. 1842, by Wm. B. Mann, J.P. Page 65.

John Green and Elizabeth Murphy, 25 Nov. 1843, by Donald Gillis, J.P. Page 65.

Elijah S. Hancock and Rebecca Bryant, 10 Nov. 1843, by John P. McNair, J.P. Page 66.

James J. Coats and Susan DuBose, 21 Dec. 1843, by J. W. Holston, minister. Page 66.

Redman Bennett and Mariand E. Grant, 7 May 1843, by Buckner Williams, J.P. Page 66.

Solomon Singleton and Angeline McNair, 11 Aug. 1842, by Wm. McCormack, J.P. Page 67.

Gideon E. Saunders and Catherine J. Henley, 31 Aug. 1842, by John A. Williams, J.P. Page 67.

Nathaniel Roach and Nancy Scarborough, 24 Dec. 1843, by Seborn J. Flake, J.P. Page 68.

Henry W. Baker and Mrs. Eliza Wheeler, 29 Dec. 1842, by Joel Sims, M.G. Page 68.

William Nowls and Sarah Ann Baugh, 27 Dec. 1842, by Jesse Tomlin, M.G. Page 69.

Deshabo Dubose and Milley Sheppard, 10 Aug. 1843, by John P. McNair, J.P. Page 69.

Jackson Austin and Brittania Cook, 2 Mar. 1843, by Wm. M. Bethune, J.P. Page 70.

Joseph Cobb and Elizabeth Cook, 7 Feb. 1843, by Wm. M. Bethune, J.P. Page 70.

Henry K. Green and Katherine McNair, 4 Jan. 1844, by Joel Sims, M.G. Page 70.

Nathan Walker and Elizabeth Dykes, 14 Apr. 1842, by John P. McNair, J.P. Page 71.

Oliver C. Patterson and Charity Herring, 7 Dec. 1843, by Wm. B. Crews, J.P. Page 71.

Abijah Reeder and Mary Atkinson, 17 Feb. 1842, by John P. McNair, J.P. Page 72.

Jesse B. Coleman and Nancy Ventress, 16 May 1843, by Joel Sims, M.G. Page 72.

John Carter and Martha Caroline Harris, 28 June 1843, by John J. Groves, M.G. Page 73.

James C. Allen and Adelade C. Gachett, 11 June 1843, by John J. Groves, M.G. Page 73.

Thomas Sheppard and Margaret Cox, 15 June 1843, by John P. McNair, J.P. Page 74.

Monro Adams and Francis E. Chany, 8 Aug. 1843, by A. Blakey, J.P. Page 74.

William Young and Elizabeth McCarrol, 5 May 1842, by J. P. McNair, J.P. Page 75.

Shadrick Sutton Stewart and Lucinda _____, 19 June 1842, by W. B. Crews, J.P. Page 75.

Hiram King and Elizabeth Hutto, 13 May 1843, by T. C. Efurd, J.P. Page 76.

William Croley and Martha Dykes, 18 May 1843, by T. C. Efurd, J.P. Page 76.

T. J. Rockmore and Sarah H. Seals, 14 Jan. 1840, by James L. Daniel, M.G. Page 77.

James Johnson and Mary Ann Caten, 16 Sept. 1841, by James L. Daniel, M.G. Page 77.

Hamilton Wade and Mary Taylor, 30 July 1843, by T. C. Efurd, J.P. Page 78.

Henry Goodwin Mitchell and Georgia Ann Virginia Mitchell, 3 May 1842, by James L. Daniel, M.G. Consent of her guardian, Randolph Mitchell, witness: Benj. J. J. Mitchell. (p. 171). Page 78.

Miles Harden and Emily Tyson, 25 Apr. 1843, by James L. Daniel, M.G. Page 79.

Council Bush and Rebecca Bushup, 20 Oct. 1843, by Jesse Tomlin, M.G. Page 79.

James E. Bennett and Lucy Catharine Lamar, 26 Jan. 1843, by

James L. Daniel, M.G.   Page 80.

Zacharia Wesly Parmer and Jane Tindell, 16 June 1842, by W. B.
Crews, J.P.   Page 80.

Murdock McNair and Sarah D. Dill, 9 Mar. 1843, by Joel Sims,
M.G.   Page 81.

Littleton Seals and Mrs. Mary Jackson, 18 May 1843, by John
Warnack, V.D.M.   Page 81.

Ezekiel Warr and Parisade Benton, 19 Apr. 1843, by John P.
McNair, J.P.   Page 82.

John Griger and Jane Doughtery, 17 July 1842, by A. Blakey, Esq.
Page 82.

Henry Hendrix and Emaline Dowling, 2 June 1842, by John W. Norton.
Page 83.

Nathaniel Knight and Dicy Huttson, 20 Jan. 1843, by M. W. Helms,
M.G.   Page 83.

Martin Taylor and Mary Ann Creel, 17 Nov. 1842, by John Williams,
J.P.   Page 84.

Francis John and Nancy Faulk, 15 June 1843, by John P. McNair,
J.P.   Page 84.

Madison Hall and Nancy Hall, 14 Mar. 1843, by J. W. Patterson.
Consent of their parents, Henry Hall and Brunt
Hall. (Groom's name given as James M. Hall in
parent's consent).   Page 85.

Henry Urquhart and Adeleline Williamson, 11 Feb. 1844, by Wm.
Head, J.P.   Page 86.

Richard Singleton and Mary Saunders, 1 Jan. 1843, by Buckner
Williams, J.P.   Page 86.

Emanuel Heath and Sarah Carrol, 15 Jan. 1843, by John P. McNair,
J.P.   Page 87.

Benjamin T. Rowe and Catharine Ann Morris, 9 Apr. 1843, by John
W. Norton.   Page 87.

Elias Lewis and Sidney D. Vickers, 2 Mar. 1843, by A. Blakey,
J.P.   Page 88.

Robert Lee and Mary Pary Parmer, 15 Dec. 1842, by Wm. B. Crews,
J.P.   Page 88.

Joseph Horn and Sarah Jane Stewart, 15 Dec. 1842, by James Buys,
M.G.   Page 89.

Felder Jo(h)nson and Julia Ellis, 29 Jan. 1843, by J. H.
Danforth, J.P.   Page 89.

Archabald McPherson and Kity Ann Tew, 19 Dec. 1842, by John P.
McNair, J.P.   Page 90.

Floyd Allums and Charlott Beasley, 29 Sept. 1842, by John P.
McNair, J.P.   Page 90.

A. W. McBeth and Emily Mann, 7 Oct. 1842, by Wm. B. Crews, J.P.
    Page 91.

Albert D. Kiels and Mahala Utsey, 18 Mar. 1843, by W. M. Shaw,
    J.P. Page 91.

Joseph Daniel, Sr. and Emeline Brooks, 14 Apr. 1842, by John W.
    Norton. Page 92.

Philip Bishop and Mary Ann Canada, 24 Nov. 1842, by Wm. M.
    McMurray. Page 92.

Philip Saunders and Narcissa Eliza Reaves, 26 Feb. 1843, by
    Peter Eldridge, M.G. Page 93.

Irvin R. Randle and Blanchy Griggs, 16 Mar. 1843, by John L.
    Groves, M.G. Page 93.

Daniel Blew and Levina Gilmer, 2 Feb. 1843, by T. C. Efurd, J.P.
    Page 94.

G. W. Edwards and Elizabeth Picket, 31 Oct. 1842, by Benjamin
    D. Sellers, J.P. Page 94.

Joseph D. Gibson and Emily Watson, 13 Oct. 1842, by Benjamin D.
    Sellers, J.P.   Consent of his guardian, Z. J.
    Babb. Page 95.

James Mills and Elphan Rains, 24 Feb. 1842, by Benjamin D.
    Sellers, J.P. Page 95.

Cary P. Woolf and Huldale Jourdon, 19 Jan. 1843, by T. C.
    Efurd, J.P. Page 96.

John Jones and Elizabeth Reaves, 31 July 1842, by Wm. B. Crews,
    J.P.   Page 96.

William Carter and Elizabeth Webb, 5 July 1842, by Wm. M.
    Bethune, J.P. Page 97.

Benjamin A. Barron and Mary Ann E. Ward, 18 Sept. 1842, by Wm.
    McCormack, J.P. Page 97.

Charles Petty and Narcissa Clark, 20 Oct. 1842, by Joel Sims,
    M.G. Page 98.

Lovard Lee and Susan E. Loveless, 24 Oct. 1842, by James Clark,
    J.P. Page 98.

Daniel Williamson and Elizabeth Smyley, 22 Jan. 1843, by A.
    Blakey, J.P. Page 99.

Isham Jourdan and Nancy Powell, 26 Dec. 1841, by Edwin James.
    Page 99.

William Camafax and Emaly Billings, 5 July 1842, by Edwin James.
    Page 100.

James Mixon and Nancy Jourden, 9 Jan. 1842, by Edwin James.
    Page 100.

Robert Dubose and Alsey Thomas, 3 Nov. 1842, by John P. McNair,
    J.P. Page 101.

9

John Robinson and Jane Baxley, 10 July 1842, by John P. McNair, J.P. Page 101.

Joseph Cook and Sidney Canada, 19 Jan. 1843, by Wm. M. McMurray. Page 102.

John R. Simmons and Martha Spears, 26 June 1842, by Buckner Williams, J.P. Page 102.

William B. Crews and Catherine McSwean, 8 Dec. 1842, by John P. McNair, J.P. Page 103.

Angus McSwean and Mary Lee, 2 Mar. 1843, by Wm. B. Crews, J.P. Page 103.

Adham Henley and Leta Williams, 15 Dec. 1842, by Solomon Sikes. Page 104.

Alley G. Hill and Sarah Early, 3 Feb. 1843, by J. H. Danforth, J.P. Page 104.

David Lewis and Milly Kerkland, 18 Aug. 1842, by A. Blakey, J.P. Page 105.

Elisha Hewling and Harrit Arrington, 19 Feb. 1843, by T. C. Efurd, J.P. Page 105.

Theophilus Aulston and Adaline Nix, 8 July 1842, by J. H. Danforth, J.P. Page 106.

James A. Kidd and Eliza Singleton, 4 Dec. 1842, by Wm. Head, J.P. Page 106.

John Mitchell and Mrs. Seala Hartzog, 13 Aug. 1843, by Henry Blanchett, J.P. Page 107.

Thomas W. White and Mary Warr, 27 July 1843, by Henry Blanchet, J.P. Page 107.

William U. Wilks and Sarah L. Jones, 10 Nov. 1842, by Wm. McCormack, J.P. Page 108.

Ezekiel Bennet and Martha Harwell, 4 May 1843, by James L. Daniel, M.G. Page 108.

L. P. Henry and Samanthy Auston, 3 Oct. 1843, by Wm. M. Shaw, J.P. Page 109.

Thomas J. Gregrory and Elizabeth Deshazo, 31 Oct. 1842, by Wm. B. Mann, J.P. Page 109.

Thomas Griggs and Mahaley Hosenback, issued 17 Feb. 1840, executed by Jas. Cadenhead, M.G. Page 110.

Elisha Worrel and Liney Coats, issued 1 May 1843, return not recorded. Page 110.

Archibald McDonald and Candis Jackson, 4 Nov. 1842, by Wm. McCormack, J.P. Page 111.

Dr. William L. Cowan and Ann S. Pugh, issued 21 Feb. 1834, executed by John W. Norton. Page 111.

Robert O. Dale and Catharine Epshaw, 31 July 1843, by Stephen
F. Pilly, Elder of M. E. Church. Page 112.

Jesse Faulk and Nancy Head, 25 July 1843, by Wm. M. McMurray,
J.P. Page 112.

John McGrude and Narcissa Briant, 28 Apr. 1842, by James L.
Daniel, M.G. Page 113.

Thomas Cox and Susan White, 24 Nov. 1843, by Henry Blanchet,
J.P. Page 113.

James H. Smith and Mary Johnson, 14 Dec. 1843, by B. Williams,
J.P. Page 114.

Mickins Spears and Mary B. Singleton, 14 Dec. 1843, by Zacheous
Nix, M.G. Page 114.

Manning H. Mann and Maria T. Mann, 21 Dec. 1843, by Zacheous
Nix, M.G. Page 115.

Lewis People and Sence Browning, 6 June 1843, by John A.
Williams, J.P. Page 115.

Zachariah Tate and Cyntha Paramore, 24 Nov. 1843, by Buckner
Williams, J.P. Page 116.

John Daniel and Elizabeth Sasser, 10 July 1842, by Joel Sims,
M.G. Page 116.

John Bennet and Eliza Whittemore, 20 Jan. 1842, by James L.
Daniel, M.G. Page 117.

Daniel G. Lewis and Lucyann Efurd, 5 Oct. 1843, by Buckner
Williams, J.P. Page 117.

Herod Whitemore and Jane P. Bell, 17 Jan. 1842, by James L.
Daniel, M.G. Page 118.

Angus McNeill and Margaret McLeod, 7 Sept. 1843, by John Warrick,
V.D.M. Page 118.

William White and Eliza Ware, 25 Oct. 1843, by Henry Blanchet,
J.P. Page 119.

James Houston and Nancy Bush, 9 Nov. 1843, by Jesse Tomlin, M.G.
Page 119.

William R. Tomlin and Marthena Parmer, 14 Nov. 1843, by Wm. B.
Mann, J.P. Page 120.

John Holland and Huldah Herrington, 14 Apr. 1844, by Wm. K.
Jones, J.P. Page 120.

Benjamin L. West made Deacon in the M. E. Church at Selma, 4
Jan. 1841, Jas. O. Andrews. Page 121.

David Spears and Serena Williamson, 11 Aug. 1844, by Thos. F.
Bludworth, J.P. Page 122.

Eli Gilmore and Caroline Desazo, 4 Aug. 1844, by Joel Sims, M.G.
Page 122.

James T. Beasley and Rebecca L. Efurd, 12 Aug. 1844, by Jesse
        Tomlin, M.G.   Page 123.

J. R. Page and Lusinda Johnson, 6 Aug. 1844, by Thos. F.
        Bludworth.   Page 123.

Thomas Doster and Elizar Laney, 3 Aug. 1844, by Appleton Haygood,
        M.G.   Page 124.

William Rouse and Mary Sutherland, 25 July 1844, by Benjamin D.
        Sellers, J.P.   Page 124.

Shaderick Williamson and Matilda Catharine McIntosh, 1 Aug. 1844,
        by W. K. Jones, J.P.   Page 125.

George Hartly and Mary Nickols, 11 June 1844, by Wesley Vinson,
        J.P.   Page 125.

John Grubbs and Lucitta Martin, issued 23 Apr. 1844, return not
        recorded.   Page 126.

John Neice and Mary Price, 14 July 1844, by Thos. F. Bludworth,
        J.P.   Page 127.

Elish Price and Nancy Neice, 14 July 1844, by Thos. F. Bludworth.
        Page 127.

Needham Lee and Ailsey Boylston, 17 Sept. 1844, by John P.
        McNair, J.P.   Page 128.

Richard E. Head and Epsey Willis, 20 Mar. 1844, by Joel Nichols.
        Page 128.

Donald Kenedy and Nancy McLean, 7 Feb. 1844, by John A.
        Williams, J.P.   Page 129.

John M. Lightner and Martha McCarty, 16 May 1844, by Jesse
        Tomlin, M.G.   Page 129.

Jesse Reader and Caroline Elizabeth Givins, 18 Apr. 1844, by
        John Helms, J.P.   Page 130.

Fulin R. Brown and Mary McUlt, 21 Mar. 1844, by Daniel Campbell,
        J.P.   Page 130.

John McMichael and Nancy Matilda Hix, 4 Apr. 1844, by T. C.
        Efurd, J.P.   Page 131.

Talbot M. Stewart and Sely Truit, 21 Jan. 1844, by Donald
        Gillis, J.P.   Page 131.

Charles P. Chaney and Lydia Jane Spears, 30 June 1844, by Rev.
        James Shanks.   Page 132.

John Q. Adams and Cloah Hays, 23 June 1844, by Benjamin D.
        Sellers, J.P.   Page 133.

John F. Rivers and Sarah F. Upshaw, issued 17 June 1844, return
        not recorded.   Page 133.

John Franklin Williamson and Mary Elin Coalson, 1 June 1844, by
        Henry Faulk, Jr., J.P.   Page 134.

Sion Creech and Nancy Spear, 1 Jan. 1844, by Wm. M. Bethune, J.P.   Page 134.

Maj. John Sanford and Narissa C. Rabb, issued 7 Aug. 1839, executed, Jas. L. Daniel, M.G.   Page 135.

William Hayes and Elizabeth J. McGowan, executed 25 Dec. 1841.   Page 135.

Thomas Lynch and Martha Allen, 27 Oct. 1842, by Stephen F. Pilly, M. E. Church.   Page 135.

Minton Shaw and Eliza Thomas, issued 15 Sept. 1842, executed.   Page 136.

Robert Carol and Elizabeth Argroves, issued 24 Sept. 1843, executed, Jno. Helms, J.P.   Page 136.

William Thomas and Elizabeth Arrington, 9 June 1845, by T. C. Efurd, J.P.   Page 137.

Colman Helms and Jane Sheppard, 15 Sept. 1844, by Aaron Helms, V.D.M.   Page 137.

Wilson B. Avent and Sarah McLendon, 19 Sept. 1844, by Wesley Vinson, J.P.   Consent of her father, John McLendon.   Page 138.

William Cook and Mary Bowen, 24 Dec. 1844, by A. M. Cobb, J.P.   Page 138.

Canady Benton Anderson and Mrs. Alice Williams, 7 Mar. 1844, by Jesse Tomlin, M.G.   Page 139.

Jacob L. Tomlin and Mary Ann Hearing, 3 Oct. 1844, by R. T. White, J.P.   Page 139.

Henry Carter and Sarah S. Cearcy, 13 Feb. 1844, by Soln. Sikes.   Page 140.

William H. Harwell and Francis Glover, 5 Nov. 1844, by Wesley Vinson, J.P.   Page 140.

Martin Roe and Caroline Scott, 5 Sept. 1844, by Joel Sims, M.G.   Page 140.

William Aplin and Elizabeth Gomillion, 18 Oct. 1844, by Joseph Aplin, J.P.   Page 141.

Colen Young and Lucinda Rachels, 31 Oct. 1844, by Wm. K. Jones, J.P.   Page 141.

James Jones and Jane Martin, 28 July 1844, by James Griffith, M.G.   Page 142.

John Shepperd and Moley Bass, 28 Nov. 1844, by Jesse Tomlin, M.G.   Page 142.

John C. Hodge and Ann Hill, 1 Dec. 1844, by J. L. Williams, J.P.   Page 143.

William Bryan and Epsey Hill, 5 Dec. 1844, by Jno. L. Williams, J.P.   Page 143.

13

Reuben J. Sims and Margaret Stripling, 5 Dec. 1844, by Zacheous
Nix, M.G. Page 143.

E. D. Carter and Katharine Ramsey, 30 Oct. 1844, by D. D.
Williams. Page 144.

Allen Sapp and Emeline Bigford, 8 Dec. 1844, by Thos. E.
Bludworth, J.P. Page 144.

Jacob Campbell and Martha Brown, 29 Dec. 1844, by David Campbell,
J.P. Page 145.

Regden Brasset and Artimisia Delafield, 12 Jan. 1845, by D.
McKenzie, J.P. Page 145.

John W. Johnston and Louisa Ball, 18 Aug. 1844, by James L.
Daniel, M.G. Page 146.

Goodman Bryant and Annis Taylor, 30 Dec. 1844, by Jesse Tomlin,
M.G. Consent of her step-father, Silas Cannon.
Page 146.

Lewis H. Rouse and Sarah Canady, 14 Dec. 1844, by Thos. F.
Bludworth, J.P. Page 147.

John Mandley and Pauline Landrum, 5 Jan. 1845, by Z. Wood, J.P.
Page 147.

Obediah Thompson and Rebecca West, issued 19 Dec. 1844, executed
by James Cadenhead. Page 148.

James R. Upshaw and Maria G. Brown, 24 Dec. 1844, by J. E. Glenn.
Page 148.

Allen T. Glenn and Jane C. Bryant, 15 Dec. 1844, by Zacheous
Nix, M.G. Page 149.

Alexander Croley and Susan Jones, 2 Jan. 1845, by P. Bludworth,
J.P. (She gave oath she was 18 years old). Page
149.

William H. Jones and Rebecca Westbrook, 17 Nov. 1844, by P.
Bludworth, J.P. Page 150.

Elijah Bolton and Amanda Briant, 16 Jan. 1845, by John L.
Williams, J.P. Page 150.

Lemuel Morrison and Leonorah Owen, 26 Jan. 1845, by Appleton
Haygood, M.G. Page 151.

John Web and Telisha Page, 9 Jan. 1845, by P. Bludworth, J.P.
Page 151.

Charnoch Jones and Nancy Sanders, 16 Jan. 1845, by Thos. F.
Bludworth, J.P. Page 151.

Israel B. Williams and Narcissa E. Morris, 14 Jan. 1845, by
Appleton Haygood, M.G. (Minister's credentials
recorded in Tuskegee). Page 152.

Tilman McCarty and Jane Loveless, 29 Jan. 1845, by Jesse Tomlin,
M.G. Page 152.

Henry R. Bostick and Elizabeth Grant, issued 21 Jan. 1845,
        executed by D. Campbell.   Page 153.

Littleton Flowers and Delilah Volentine, 8 Feb. 1845, by Wm. G.
        Stephen, J.P.   Page 153.

Archibald Campbell and Polly Jane Stephens, 11 Feb. 1845, by D.
        McKenzie.   Page 153.

Sherwood L. Stanley and Nancy An Martin, 16 Jan. 1845, by B. F.
        Pearson, J.P.   Page 154.

William Day and Sarah Dill, issued 4 Feb. 1845, executed by
        Daniel Campbell, J.P.   Page 154.

B. F. Petty and Catherine Smith, 20 Feb. 1845, by Joel Sims,
        M.G.   Page 155.

Isaac Burnett and Matilda Kelly, 13 Mar. 1845, by R. S. White,
        J.P.   Page 155.

Thomas W. Richards and Temperance Smith, 14 Sept. 1843, by Soln.
        Sikes.   Page 156.

Gideon Bowden and Poly Ann Floyd, 5 Nov. 1844, by Jesse Tomlin,
        M.G.   Page 156.

Needham Bryant and Elizabeth Eckols, 11 May 1843, by James Buys,
        M.G.   Page 157.

Gideon Gordy and Rebecca Head, issued 19 Jan. 1845, return not
        recorded.   Page 157.

Robert Tillman and Mrs. Nancy Casy, 1 Apr. 1845, by D. McKenzie,
        J.P.   Page 158.

Middleton Dubose and Susanah Barfield, 16 Feb. 1845, by J. W.
        Holston, M.G.   Page 158.

John M. Head and Lurceny Cane, 17 Nov. 1844, by William Payne,
        M.G.   Page 159.

Wilson Curiton and Mary Walls, 4 July 1844, by Wesley Vinson,
        J.P.   Page 159.

Francis S. Howard and Kisiah Faulk, 23 May 1844, by Daniel
        Campbell, J.P.   Page 160.

John T. Grubbs and Lucilla Martin, issued 23 Apr. 1844, return
        not recorded.   Page 160.

John G. Williams and Christian McLean, 23 Mar. 1845, by Wm. B.
        Crews, J.P.   Page 161.

Hardy Bass and Lucinda Price, 17 Apr. 1845, by Jesse Tomlin, M.G.
        Page 162.

John Givins and Mary Jane Bairfield, issued 17 May 1845, executed
        by John Cox, J.P.   Page 163.

William H. Thornton and Mary B. Shorter, 10 Apr. 1845, by James
        Mathews.   Page 163.

Andrew H. Beauchamp and Sarah A. Lowman, 28 May 1845, by J. W. Holston, M.G. Page 164.

George W. Rice and Amanda Miles, 20 Apr. 1845, by Z. J. Daniel, J.P. Page 164.

John E. Lowman and Mary Norton, 21 Sept. 1843, by John Hunter, M.G. Page 165.

Andrew Jackson Miller and Elizabeth Ann Faulk, 8 Oct. 1843, by Henry Faulk, Jr., J.P. Page 165.

George Barefoot and Arman Teader, 1 June 1845, by David Campbell, J.P. Page 166.

Robert N. Jones and Mrs. Penelope Pope, 6 Mar. 1845, by Wesley Vinson, J.P. Page 166.

John Garris and Susan Watson, 2 Feb. 1845, by Benjamin D. Sellers, J.P. Page 166.

William J. Ranton and Caroline Kemp, 25 Jan. 1845, by Wesley Vinson, J.P. Page 167.

James Bottoms and Nancy Willice, 11 Feb. 1845, by Benjamin D. Sellers, J.P. Page 167.

William Reynolds and Mrs. Sarah Tatte, 9 Apr. 1845, by W. R. Jones, J.P. Page 168.

Daniel R. Thomas and Eliza Pattison, 2 Jan. 1845, by Wm. R. Jones, J.P. Page 168.

George W. Faulk and Margarett Webb, 27 Mar. 1845, by Wesley Vinson, J.P. Page 169.

Simon A. Sheppard and Mary E. Beasley, 22 Dec. 1845, by Wesley Vinson, J.P. Page 169.

William Jernigan and Martha Deshazo, 12 Mar. 1845, by W. R. Jones, J.P. Page 170.

R. J. Cooper and Sary Ann Austin, 24 Dec. 1844, by Peyton Bludworth, J.P. Page 170.

John Boswell James and Mary E. Brizzell, 8 May 1845, by Henry Faulk, Jr., J.P. Page 170.

William H. Carter and Sarah M. Harris, 3 Nov. 1844, by John J. Groves, M.G. Page 172.

Snoden Karklin and Aily Bass, 20 Sept. 1844, by Henry Blanchet, J.P. Page 172.

Barnabas B. Baxley and Mary Robson, 14 Nov. 1844, by Wm. J. Stephens, J.P. Page 173.

William Cox and Harriet Casey, 1 June 1843, by Wm. M. Shaw. Page 173.

David J. Creder and Drucilla Jackson, 12 Oct. 1843, by Joseph Aplin, J.P. Page 173.

Hampton Casey and Elizabeth Cotton, 17 July 1844, by Joel Sims, M.G. Page 174.

Hybert King and Mary Ziterow, 29 Aug. 1844, by P. Bludworth, J.P. Page 174.

Jackson Hagler and Malinda Helms, 14 Mar. 1844, by Aaron Helms, V.D.M. Page 175.

William B. Pope and Elizabeth Jones, 30 Oct. 1844, by Benjamin D. Sellers, J.P. Page 175.

Edwin Willis and Mrs. Matilda Boit, issued 27 Nov. 1844, return not recorded. Page 176.

James H. L. Sanders and Mary Barry, 5 June 1845, by Jesse Tomlin, M.G. Page 177.

Early D. Avesett and Ann Eliza Avesett, 24 Oct. 1844, by Wesley Vinson, J.P. Consent of her father, Mathew Avesett. Page 177.

Abram B. Starke and Francis H. Jackson, 8 Oct. 1844, by James L. Daniel, M.G. Page 178.

John B. Bizzell and Mary Adams, 12 Nov. 1844, by Daniel Campbell, J.P. Page 178.

Joel A. Sims and Elizabeth Garrett, 15 Oct. 1843, by Zacheous Nix, M.G. Page 179.

David Spear and Sarah Adeline Chany, 19 Nov. 1843, by A. Blakey, J.P. Page 179.

William J. G. Barry and Selety Carroll, 17 Mar. 1845, by Zacheous Nix, M.G. Page 180.

Henry Carrol and Theresa Ann Elizabeth Fleming, 29 May 1845, by W. J. Stephens, J.P. Page 180.

Rairden Newman and Elizabeth Jane Lawrence, 25 May 1845, by R. T. White, J.P. Page 180.

Henry S. Faulk and Sarah J. Bizzell, 29 Jan. 1845, by Henry Faulk, Jr., J.P. Page 181.

Levi L. Daniel and Ellen E. Aspinwall, 8 July 1845, by James L. Daniel, M.G. Page 181.

Thomas S. Lightner and Mary Bishop, 16 July 1845, by Jesse Tomlin, M.G. Page 182.

George C. Taylor and Hetty M. Cropp, 21 Aug. 1845, by J. E. Glenn. Page 182.

Owen Eidson and Mary Jane Herring, 17 July 1845, by Jesse Tomlin, M.G. Page 183.

William G. Bush and Mary Allen, 25 June 1845, by Wm. B. Crews, J.P. Page 183.

Emanuel Thomas and Mrs. Martha Thomas, 1 Sept. 1845, by Aaron Helms, V.D.M. Page 184.

John B. Appling and Laura R. A. Wiley, 29 Sept. 1845, by R. C. Smith, M.G. Page 184.

John T. Martin and Hepsey Worthington, 11 May 1845, by T. C. Efurd, J.P. Page 185.

James Tew and Lavinia Wilkinson, 5 Oct. 1845, by John Cox, J.P. Page 185.

James C. Wheeler and Elizabeth Hays, 21 Sept. 1845, by Wm. M. Bethune, J.P. Page 186.

William G. Bush and Mary Williams, 15 Oct. 1845, by Wm. K. Jones, J.P. Page 186.

Samuel Benton and Mariana Johnson, 18 July 1845, by D. McKenzie, J.P. Page 187.

Obadiah Florence and Aramitta Pitts, 8 June 1843, by James L. Daniel, M.G. Page 187.

William M. Renfroe and Elizabeth A. Hudson, 24 Nov. 1844, by Jas. L. Daniel, M.G. Page 188.

Martin Bollabough and Elizabeth Aulston, 19 June 1845, by James B. Johnston, J.P. Page 188.

Green Heath and Bethena Flowers, 28 Sept. 1845, by Wm. J. Stephens, J.P. Page 189.

Levi G. Bright and Emeline Scarborough, 17 July 1845, by Wesley Vinson, J.P. Page 189.

John T. Williams and Elizabeth Kemp, 13 May 1845, by Wesley Vinson, J.P. Page 190.

George M. T. Caton and Penlope D. Thompson, 14 Aug. 1845, by James Buys, M.G. Consent of his father, John D. Caton. Page 191.

Joshua Baker and Sarah Filimgam, 23 Oct. 1845, by D. McKenzie, J.P. Page 191.

Ichabod B. Summerlin and Rhoda Curinton, 27 Oct. 1845, by M. Avent, J.P. Page 191.

Daniel Danford and Dorothea Jane Miller, 26 Oct. 1845, by P. Bludworth, J.P. Page 192.

Jonathan Moats and Nancy Ann Harveston, 30 Sept. 1845, by Peyton Bludworth. Page 192.

Jonathan R. Lampley and Catherine A. Whiddon, 16 Oct. 1845, by Peyton Bludworth, J.P. Page 193.

Alfred J. Glover and Elizabeth Sheppard, 6 Apr. 1843, by Charles Evans, M.G. Page 193.

William Morgan and Caroline Harvey Jenkins, 10 Aug. 1845, by John G. Cowan, M.G. Page 194.

John A. Rogers and Polly Ann Reves, 23 Sept. 1845, by W. B. Crews, J.P. Page 194.

Michael P. Vickers and Sarah Ann E. Wall, 18 Sept. 1845, by W. B.
          Crews, J.P.   Page 195.

Thomas J. Glover and Rachael Vinning, 5 Oct. 1845, by John G.
          Cowan, M.G.   Page 195.

James Spruel and Catherine Bush, 18 Nov. 1845, by R. T. White,
          J.P.   Page 196.

Simon G. Hammock and Caroline Jane Hammock, 15 Oct. 1843, by D.
          Gillis, J.P.   Page 196.

Irvin Elkins and Sarah Bently, 23 Oct. 1845, by Jesse Tomlin,
          M.G.   Page 197.

James Crosley and Mary Ann E. Morgan, 18 Nov. 1845, by L. C.
          Harrison, M.G.   Consent of his guardian, E. C.
          Holloman.   Page 197.

Jesse Jamison and Lavonia Courson, 20 Dec. 1845, by R. T. White,
          J.P.   Page 198.

Robert T. Tate and Eliza Craft, 4 Dec. 1845, by Wm. K. Jones,
          J.P.   Page 198.

Thomas Miffin and Charity Thomas, 28 Dec. 1845, by Wm. K. Jones,
          J.P.   Page 199.

R. C. Brigman and Sarah Ann Lovett, 29 Dec. 1845, by D. McKenzie,
          J.P.   Page 199.

John M. Foster and Malinda Wingat, 25 Dec. 1845, by Henry Faulk,
          Jr., J.P.   Page 200.

Milton Reaves and Mary Tillman, 11 Dec. 1846, by Henry Faulk,
          Jr., J.P.   Page 200.

Nathaniel Raeley and Sarah Ann Pate, 30 Dec. 1845, by Daniel
          Campbell, J.P.   Page 201.

Reubin Sauls and Elizabeth Raeley, 30 Dec. 1845, by Daniel
          Campbell, J.P.   Page 201.

Benjamin Carter and Drucilla Jan Deleshaw, 9 Dec. 1845, by
          Daniel Campbell, J.P.   Page 202.

Wesley Bodyford and Jane Turner, 21 Dec. 1845, by Solomon Sikes,
          minister.   Page 202.

H. L. Jourdan and Ann E. Seals, 24 Jan. 1845, by Andrew Cumbie,
          minister.   Page 203.

Samuel Strange and Polly Ann Burnham, 4 Jan. 1846, by Z. Wood,
          J.P.   Page 203.

John McLendon and Nancy Ann Owen, 11 Jan. 1846, by Thos. F.
          Bludworth, J.P.   Page 204.

James Costen and Annis Bryant, 29 Jan. 1846, by Thos. F.
          Bludworth, J.P.   Page 204.

Alfred Harrison and Catherine Blanchet, 9 Jan. 1846, by James
          Shanks, J.P.   Consent of his mother, Elizabeth

Harrison. Page 205.

Asher Reaves and Nelly Parmer, 17 Dec. 1845, by Wm. B. Crews,
J.P. Page 205.

Austin H. Turner and Martha L. Brown, 2 Jan. 1846, by John G.
Cowan, M.G. Page 206.

John W. Gallaway and Mahala Lewis, 11 Jan. 1846, by Z. J. Daniel,
J.P. Page 206.

Timothy Lee and Nancy Palmer, 14 Nov. 1845, by J. W. Holston,
M.G. Page 207.

Phillip Raiford and Hester Elizabeth Horn, 8 Jan. 1846, by
J. W. Holston, M.G. Page 207.

Daniel A. Adkinson and Larkey Ludlum, 11 Dec. 1845, by Wm. J.
Stephens, J.P. Page 208.

William R. Kilpatrick and Elizabeth Jane Benson, 25 Dec. 1845,
by Wm. J. Stephens, J.P. Page 208.

Samuel Pitits and Jeanette Margaret Floyd, 12 Jan. 1846, by
Daniel Campbell, J.P. Page 209.

Sempson Lindsey and Martha Jane Beasley, 8 Jan. 1846, by D.
McKenzie, J.P. Page 209.

Russel Jones and Elizaneth McDonald, 13 Jan. 1846, by M. A.
Patterson, M.G. Page 210.

John G. Cowan ordained as minister at the meeting at the
Primitive Baptist Church in Barbour County on 21
June 1845. Presbytery: Jesse Tomlin, P. H.
Edwards & Willis S. Jarrell. Page 210.

Robert Campbell and Ana Bryant, 15 Feb. 1846, by Daniel
Campbell, J.P. Page 211.

William Ivy and Zelpha Ann Elizabeth McDonald, 24 Feb. 1846, by
Appleton Haygood, M.G. Consent of her guardian,
N. McDonald. Page 212.

Calvin E. Harden and Mary Ann Rollins, 21 Sept. 1846, by James
M. Warrick, M.G. Page 212.

John W. Elmer and Caracey Eliza Demsey, 24 Aug. 1845, by James
B. Johnson, J.P. Page 213.

Joshua H. Alston and Sarah Moore, 10 Oct. 1845, by James S.
Johnson, J.P. Page 213.

Daniel C. Scott and Mary H. F. Wellborn, 19 Feb. 1846, by G.
Malone, M.G.

Samuel Oliver and Nancy Ann Matilda Cox, 26 Feb. 1846, by Cary
Curry, M.G. Page 214.

Wiley G. Harris and Mary An E. Mitchell, issued 28 May 1844,
return not recorded. Page 215.

Hansford Bodiford and Nancy McKithren, 18 Oct. 1845, by John A.

20

Williams, J.P.   Page 215.

Sterling Davis and Francis Byrd, 31 Dec. 1845, by John A.
Williams, J.P.   Page 216.

Henry P. Calhoun and Mrs. Rebecca Calhoun, 30 Oct. 1845, by
Wesley Vinson, J.P.   Page 216.

William M. Hawkins and Ann Cornelia Mills, 24 Nov. 1845, by
R. C. Smith, M.G.   Page 217.

William Haley and Mrs. Emily Canifax, 22 Dec. 1845, by R. C.
Smith, M.G.   Page 217.

Hugh A. Blount and Susan Magruder, 30 Dec. 1845, by R. C.
Smith, M.G.   Page 218.

Alexander McRae and Eliza Westbrook, 24 Dec. 1845, by M. A.
Patterson, M.G.   Page 218.

Needham B. Sutton and Amanday Caroline E. Campbell, 12 Mar.
1846, by Henry Faulk, Jr., J.P.   Page 219.

Ebenezer Frasier and Jane Ball, 26 Mar. 1846, by Daniel
Campbell, J.P.   Page 219.

George W. McRae and Christian McLeod, 20 Feb. 1845, by James
Shanks.   Page 220.

William Peebles and Clarcey M. Nowland, 5 Feb. 1846, by Solomon
Sikes, M.G.   Page 220.

William Prescot and Catherine Jones, 24 Feb. 1846, by Jno. L.
Williams, J.P.   Page 221.

William Loflin and Martha Johnson, 5 Mar. 1846, by Wesley
Vinson, J.P.   Page 221.

Green B. Coxwell and Emily Rowland, 21 Feb. 1846, by Wesley
Vinson, J.P.   Consent of her father, Thomas
Rowland.   Page 222.

John C. Weaver and Mrs. Nancy M. Beauchamp, 5 Feb. 1846, by
J. W. Holston, M.G.   Page 222.

Major B. Sykes and Elizabeth Barry, 9 Apr. 1846, by John A.
Williams, J.P.   Page 223.

G. A. Roberts and Nancy A. Oliver, 20 May 1846, by R. C. Smith,
M.G.   Page 223.

B. F. Dogget and Miss D. Yarborough, 19 Feb. 1846, by James L.
Daniel, M.G.   Page 224.

Reesey Hutson and Sarah Ann Carter, 3 May 1846, by Daniel
Campbell, J.P.   Page 224.

Aranton H. H. Phillips and Marthey A. Sutton, 16 Apr. 1846, by
Henry Faulk, Jr., J.P.   Page 225.

James Mulchaby and Charity Thomas, 2 June 1846, by James Clark,
J.P.   Page 226.

James Ventress and Mary Jane Dill, 4 June 1846, by Joel Sims, M.G. Page 226.

John W. McAlister and Julia Hyat, 21 May 1846, by N. D. Scales. Page 227.

Jordan J. Smith and Mary Ann Clark, 12 June 1846, by Edwin James, M.G. Page 227.

Thomas Smith and Priscello Flowers, 16 Apr. 1846, by Wm. J. Stephens, J.P. Page 228.

Reubin R. Young and Caroline Sims, 24 June 1846, by Wm. J. Stephens, J.P. Page 228.

Arthur Lott and Amanda Young, 24 June 1846, by Wm. J. Stephens, J.P. Consent of her father, William Young. Page 229.

Thomas Harrod and Meranda Kelly, 16 July 1846, by Jno. L. Williams, J.P. Page 230.

William R. Crumby and Mary E. Wellborn, 6 May 1846, by L. C. Harrison, M.G. Page 230.

Jeptha Lindsey and Mrs. Lydia Ann Register, 5 Aug. 1846, by Wm. B. Crews, J.P. Page 231.

Stephen Hughs and Mrs. Nelly Ginwright, 3 May 1846, by Council Bush, J.P. Page 231.

Harrell Flowers and Julia Bush, 8 July 1846, by Wm. B. Crews, J.P. Page 232.

James McGilbery and Anna McNeill, 4 July 1846, by Wm. B. Crews, J.P. Page 232.

John R. Fergof and Jincy Flowers, 14 May 1846, by Wm. B. Crews, J.P. Page 233.

Tappy Troublefield and Harriet Highsmith. 19 June 1846, by Wm. B. Crews, J.P. Page 233.

Edmond G. Willis and Missourie A. Baker, 2 Aug. 1846, by B. F. Pearson, J.P. Page 234.

John Dobbs and Elizabeth Creech, 1 Feb. 1846, by Wm. M. Bethune, J.P. Page 234.

Edward C. Bullock and Mary J. Snipes, 29 Oct. 1845, by J. L. Gay, M.G. Page 235.

David Lore and Ann P. Singleton, 1 June 1846, by Z. J. Daniel, J.P. Page 235.

John Fletcher and Martha Chester, 18 Aug. 1846, by A. C. Van Epps, J.P. Page 236.

William B. Bowden and Eliza W. Cenada, 13 Aug. 1846, by Wm. B. Crews, J.P. Page 236.

William W. Sims and Caroline McMurray, 27 Aug. 1846, by James Clark, J.P. Page 237.

William H. Jackson and Louisa E. Baker, 19 May 1846, by Appleton
      Haygood, M.G. Page 237.

William R. Prewitt and R. Ann Augusta Coleman, 4 Aug. 1846, by
      John J. Groves, M.G. Page 238.

John Johnson and Elizabeth Ann Bryan, 30 Sept. 1846, by R. T.
      White, J.P. Page 238.

Micajah Long and Matilda Squires, 30 Aug. 1846, by Thos. F.
      Bludworth, J.P. Page 239.

Peter Waters and Coudes Francis Hicks, 7 Aug. 1846, by James B.
      Johnson, J.P. Page 239.

James D. Stanaland and Melisse A. Connelly, 16 Aug. 1846, by
      James B. Johnson, J.P. Page 240.

Columbus Hudspeth and Ann Jane Roads, 5 Aug. 1846, by G. W.
      Purnell, M.G. Page 240.

William T. Wells and Sarah Ann Roads, 26 July 1846, by G. W.
      Purnell, M.G. Page 241.

Gilbert McCall and Adeline Warren, 24 Sept. 1846, by Reubin E.
      Brown, M.G. Page 241.

Joseph Salsbury and Mary S. Rennon, 1 July 1846, by James A.
      Heard. Page 242.

Dexter B. Tompson and Mrs. Louisa W. Spurals, 9 June 1846, by
      James A. Heard. Page 242.

Foster Robinson and Eliza Lee, 1 Oct. 1846, by James A. Heard.
      Page 243.

William Crocker and Catherine Beryhill, 1 Oct. 1846, by P.
      Bludworth, J.P.   Consent of his father, Cary
      Crocker, and her father, J. S. Beryhill. Page 244.

Alison Gist and Martha Allums, 2 July 1846, by Henry Faulk, Jr.,
      J.P. Page 245.

Nehemiah J. Moore and Rebeca E. Pinson, 10 Oct. 1846, by James
      A. Heard. Page 245.

Andrew Cumbie ordained at Bethel Baptist Church and authorized
      to preach the Gospel, 9 Nov. 1833. Crymes White,
      Barnabas Strickling & Epram Strickling. Recorded
      3 Nov. 1846. Page 246.

John Sykes and Sarah Miller, 4 June 1846, by John A. Williams,
      J.P. Page 246.

Thomas McMahan and Fanny Phillips, 23 Aug. 1846, by Peter
      Stewart, J.P. Page 247.

William J. Rolin and Sarah Jane Watson, 11 Oct. 1846, by Daniel
      Campbell, J.P. Page 247.

James Orr and Jane Bush, 20 Aug. 1846, by Council Bush, J.P.
      Consent of her father, Moses Bush. Page 248.

Joseph Henderson and Margarett McDonald, 27 Oct. 1846, by P. Bludworth, J.P. Page 249.

James R. Hill and Elizabeth Cunningham, 13 Sept. 1846, by Jno. L. Williams, J.P. Page 249.

Redding Huggins and Francis McCoy, 12 Nov. 1846, by R. E. Brown, M.G. Page 250.

William J. Bush and Mary Pugh, 16 Nov. 1846, by Council Bush, J.P. Page 250.

Alexander Campbell and Sarah Cox, 18 Nov. 1846, by Daniel Campbell, J.P. Page 251.

John Welsh and Caroline Campbell, 29 Nov. 1846, by D. McKenzie, J.P. Page 251.

Asa T. Miller and Elizabeth B. Taver, 1 Dec. 1846, by R. E. Brown, M.G. Page 252.

Abraham Pyle and Martha D. Keen, 22 Oct. 1846, by Andrew Cumbie, M.G. Page 252.

Thomas Loflin and Katherine Lochala, 2 July 1846, by Wesley Vinson, J.P. Page 253.

Thomas Green and Sarah Edge, 2 Dec. 1846, by Peyton Bludworth, J.P. Page 253.

Thomas F. Baxter and Mary Ann McLean, 6 Dec. 1846, by P. Bludworth, J.P. Page 254.

Green A. Shelby and Harriet Kenady, 10 Dec. 1846, by Thos. F. Bludworth, J.P. Page 254.

G. W. Lowman and Julia K. Treadwell, 28 July 1846, by J. W. Holston, M.G. Page 255.

Jesse Clements and Lupyna Pynes, 27 Dec. 1846, by Council Bush, J.P. Page 255.

George C. Jones and Matilda Bush, 27 Dec. 1846, by Council Bush, J.P. Page 256.

James Johnston and Harriet A. Crews, 17 Dec. 1846, by Council Bush, J.P. Page 256.

Alfred Newson and Sarah E. Newbery, 17 Dec. 1846, by T. C. Efurd, J.P. Page 257.

Isaac D. Kilpatrick and Mary M. Loveless, 23 Dec. 1846, by T. C. Efurd, J.P. Consent of her father, Benjamin D. Loveless, for his daughter to intermarry. Pages 257 & 258.

Solomon Sykes and Nancy Gibson, 31 Dec. 1846, by John J. Groves, M.G. Page 258.

Robert L. Hines and Mary Pilander, 29 Dec. 1846, by Wm. M. Bethune, J.P. Page 259.

William L. Gary and Sarah F. Trammell, 31 Dec. 1846, by Wm. B.

Bethune, J.P.   Page 259.

George W. Crymes and Mrs. Elmyra J. Lewis, 15 Dec. 1846, by
          Nicholas P. Scales, M.G.   Page 260.

Hansford Dowling and Martha Weaver, 26 Jan. 1847, by John L.
          Williams, J.P.   Page 260.

Malcom Gilchrist and Eliza J. Head, 31 Dec. 1846, by Zacheous
          Nix, M.G.   Page 261.

James M. Watkins and Melinda Hawkins, 21 Jan. 1847, by Z. J.
          Daniel, J.P.   Page 261.

Andrew J. Smith and Sarah Nixon, 28 Jan. 1847, by Z. J. Daniel,
          J.P.   Page 262.

Hiram Millsap and Martha Brown, 21 Jan. 1847, by Reuben E.
          Brown, M.G.   Page 262.

B. T. Deshazo and Laura Creech, 7 Feb. 1847, by R. T. White,
          J.P.   Page 263.

Asa Holt and Mellessa H. Glenn, 7 Jan. 1847, by J. E. Glenn.
          Page 263.

William H. Lamar and Ann M. Glenn, 7 Jan. 1847, by J. E. Glenn.
          Page 264.

Benjamin H. Waller and Rhody C. Moore, 23 Feb. 1847, by Thos.
          F. Bludworth, J.P.   Page 264.

Benjamin A. Davis and Mary Nowland, 28 Jan. 1847, by Wm. Lee,
          M.G.   Page 265.

Ezekiel Deal and Mary E. Bailey, 2 Feb. 1847, by J. W. Holston,
          M.G.   Page 265.

Thomas Harrison and Mary Dorman, 16 Feb. 1847, by P. Bludworth,
          J.P.   Page 266.

John Fulton and Mary Ann Joiner, 22 Jan. 1847, by P. Bludworth,
          J.P.   Page 266.

Lewis Hall and Jemima Reader, 10 Mar. 1847, by W. N. Atkinson,
          J.P.   Page 267.

James M. Head and Mary Jane Hall, 10 Dec. 1846, by B. F.
          Pearson, J.P.   Page 267.

Daniel M. Trammell and Mary Jane Carr, 31 Jan. 1847, by B. F.
          Pearson, J.P.   Page 268.

David Powell and Mrs. Eady Lewis, 7 Feb. 1847, by Council Bush,
          J.P.   Page 268.

William B. Allen and Caroline Commins, 20 Jan. 1847, by
          Council Bush, J.P.   Page 269.

Dr. Stirling Bass and Mary Freeman, 20 Apr. 1847, by J. E.
          Glenn.   Page 269.

Thomas Creel and Rebecca Adkinson, 9 Apr. 1847, by W. J. Stephens,

J.P.   Page 270.

Josiah Padget and Mary Ann Glass, 9 Apr. 1847, by A. T. Spence,
J.P.   Page 270.

Levi Adkins and Elizabeth Ellis, 13 Feb. 1847, by A. C. Van Epps,
J.P.   Page 271.

Barney Stephens and Eliza Brady, 24 Jan. 1847, by A. C. Van Epps,
J.P.   Page 271.

Jackson Lewis and Sarah An Mulford, 7 Feb. 1847, by Z. J.
Daniel, J.P.   Page 272.

Wiley Roberts and Sarah An Lewis, 9 Feb. 1847, by Z. J. Daniel,
J.P.   Page 273.

John A. Simpson and Sarah Ann McCoy, 15 Oct. 1846, by R. E.
Brown, M.G.   Page 273.

Jefferson A. Vining and Elizabeth Fry, 9 May 1847, by John G.
Cowan, M.G.   Page 274.

James J. Calhoun and Ann Whitehurst, 3 June 1847, by Wilson C.
Williams.   Page 274.

John C. Cawley and Virginia W. Cowart, 4 July 1847, by Andrew
Cumbie, M.G.   Page 275.

Auson T. Traywick and Margarett McMillian, 1 July 1847, by
Thomas Cargile, J.P.   Page 275.

James W. Thomas and Mary Traywick, 3 June 1847, by Thomas
Cargile, J.P.   Page 276.

Benjamin McHenry and Mrs. Milly Lewis, 30 July 1847, by G. W.
Williams, J.P.   Page 276.

Hardy Bass and Clarkey Adeline Long, 20 July 1847, by Jesse
Tomlin, M.G.   Page 277.

Benjamin Burssey and Melinda Moseley, 11 Aug. 1847, by Amos
Rist, J.P.   Page 277.

James L. Pugh and Sarah S. Hunter, 1 Nov. 1846, by R. C. Smith,
M.G.   Page 278.

Milton B. Nash and Melissa Moore, 25 Feb. 1847, by R. C. Smith,
M.G.   Page 278.

John D. Worrell and Jane Crews, 27 July 1847, by Wm. P. Miller,
M.G.   Page 279.

Henry Key, of Russell County, and Caroline G. Persons, Barbour
County, 13 July 1847, by G. W. Carter.   Page 279.

Vincent A. Tharp and Martha M. C. Curzer, 2 June 1847, by Henry
Faulk, Jr., J.P.   Page 280.

Nathan G. Waller and Emily E. Commander, 14 Sept. 1847, by Thos.
Bludworth, J.P.   Page 280.

Temple C. Millsapp and Emma E. Standley, 21 Sept. 1847, by

John J. Groves, M.G.   Page 281.

Noah H. Parramore and Melial Fillingam, 8 Sept. 1847, by Jno. L.
        Williams, J.P.   Page 281.

Calvin Shelby and Elizabeth E. Johnson, 30 Sept. 1847, by Thos.
        F. Bloodworth, J.P.   Page 282.

Thomas S. Lock and Mary P. Ryan, 26 Aug. 1847, by Geo. W.
        Williams, J.P.   Page 282.

Bennett Spears and Elizabeth Bowdon, 19 Sept. 1847, by James
        Orr, J.P.   Page 283.

James Casey and Mary Bishop, 24 Sept. 1847, by Thos. F.
        Bludworth, J.P.   Page 283.

John Black and Mary Jane Billings, 16 Sept. 1847, by O. R. Blue,
        M.G.   Page 284.

Trgan Carr and Lacy Ann Homes, 23 Sept. 1847, by Daniel Campbell,
        J.P.   Page 284.

William Hollen and Lucy Ann Brown, 27 Sept. 1847, by Daniel
        Campbell, J.P.   Page 285.

William F. Riley and Harriet Campbell, 20 Oct. 1847, by Daniel
        Campbell, J.P.   Page 285.

James K. Faulk and Mary Phillips, 9 Sept. 1847, by Henry Faulk,
        J.P.   Page 286.

Caleb Fleming and Colen Tew, 22 Sept. 1847, by W. N. Atkinson,
        J.P.   Page 286.

Henry Padget and Maria Boyd, 3 Oct. 1847, by A. T. Spence, J.P.
        Page 287.

William E. Adeir and Martha Parker, 14 Sept. 1847, by John
        Crowell, M.G.   Page 287.

Elfreda E. Rosenburg and Grbriel R. Capers, 9 Sept. 1847, by
        J. W. Holston, M.G.   Page 288.

George W. Lunsford and Mrs. Nancy Ann Blount, issued 12 July
        1847, executed.   Page 288.

Noel R. Lee and Sarah Segars, 17 Feb. 1845, by P. Bludworth,
        J.P.   Page 289.

Willis Flowers and Anna Barry, 29 Sept. 1847, by Wm. J.
        Stephens, J.P.   Page 289.

Jesse Benton and Catherine Morrison, 15 Sept. 1847, by James
        Shanks, J.P.   Page 290.

Willis B. Scrimpsher and Anna M. Bass, 25 Oct. 1847, by James
        Shanks, J.P.   Page 290.

John M. Lampley and Milly Warren, 22 June 1847, by O. D. McNeely,
        M.G.   Page 291.

William L. Brown and Sealy Ann Williams, 7 Oct. 1847, by Jesse

Tomlin, M.G.   Page 291.

John W. McAllister and Eudosia Herring, 4 Nov. 1847, by O. R. Blue, M.G.   Page 292.

John McNair and Mary Ann Grubs, 23 July 1847, by Joseph Riley, J.P.   Page 292.

Eli M. Danford and Elizabeth W. Brown, 23 Nov. 1847, by William T. Shanks.   Page 293.

Henry Graves and Mrs. Rhody Tompson, 7 Dec. 1847, by David Campbell, J.P.   Page 293.

William R. Kenady and Clary S. Thigpen, 2 Dec. 1847, by Robert Toler, M.G.   Page 294.

John C. Ussery and Mary Ann Paterson, 14 Nov. 1847, by James Orr, J.P.   Page 294.

Nelson Walkley and Ann Gardner, 28 Dec. 1846, by R. C. Smith, M.G.   Page 295.

Aretus W. Jones and Mary Bush, 23 Dec. 1847, by James Orr. Page 295.

Neel Gillis and Nancy Herring, 11 Nov. 1847, by James Orr. Page 296.

Richard J. West and Sealy Killingworth, 23 Dec. 1847, by Thomas J. Head, J.P.   Page 296.

George W. Richards and Mary Ann Grubbs, 11 Nov. 1847, by James Orr.   Page 297.

Daniel Gilchrist and Elizabeth Williamson, 13 Dec. 1847, by Peter Stewart, J.P.   Page 297.

Alex C. Stephens and Nancy Norton, 30 Nov. 1847, by Saul Armstrong, M.G.   Page 298.

William Barham and Mary Turman, 15 Oct. 1847, by John J. Groves, M.G.   Page 298.

Osborn Stone and Nancy Flournoy, 28 Dec. 1847, by John Groves, M.G.   Consent of her father, James Flournoy. Witness: James E. Flournoy.   Page 299.

James E. Flournoy and Charity Johnson, 26 Dec. 1847, by A. T. Spence, J.P.   Page 300.

Washington F. Drake and Mahany Lewis, 28 Dec. 1847, by R. E. Brown, M.G.   Page 300

A. S. Flournoy and Sarah A. M. Johnson, 5 Jan. 1848, by Thos. F. Bludworth, J.P.   Page 301.

Allen Harp and Emeline Arington, 6 Jan. 1848, by Thos. F. Bludworth, J.P.   Page 301.

Thomas J. Head and Frances Johnson, 6 Jan. 1848, by Thos. F. Bludworth, J.P.   Page 302.

Shearman Cox and Ann Maria Westbrook, 5 Dec. 1847, by Rev. W.
Wilks. Page 302.

John Brazzil and Emily Dellafield, 15 Jan. 1848, by W. M. Shaw,
J.P. Page 303.

William L. Loveless and Lucy Ann Warren, 18 Jan. 1848, by Amos
Rist, J.P. Page 303.

William Miles and Charity Griffin, 28 Dec. 1847, by Thomas
Cargile, J.P. Page 304.

Mathew M. Laseter and Jane Bishop, 30 Dec. 1847, by Jesse Tomlin,
M.G. Consent of his father, Mathew Laseter, and
her mother, Nancy Bishop. Pages 304 & 305.

William Kelly and Sarah Heath, 23 Dec. 1847, by Jesse Tomlin,
M.G. Consent of her father, Isaac Heath. Pages
305 & 306.

G. B. Bush and Nancy Jane Walls, 6 Jan. 1848, by James Orr, J.P.
Page 306.

William A. Horn and Masouria Caroline Spurlock, 23 Jan. 1848, by
Solomon Sikes, D.D. Page 306.

Tobias Williams and Sarah Maria Sercy, 4 Nov. 1847, by Solomon
Sikes, D.D. Page 306.

John McDowell and Martha A. Jones, 6 Feb. 1848, by W. Wilks.
Page 307.

David Johnson and Mary A. Holder, 3 Feb. 1848, by Thos. F.
Bludworth, J.P. Page 307.

Jeol Brunson and Mary Hickman, 6 Jan. 1848, by A. J. Wilson, J.P.
Consent of her mother, Polly Hickman. Page 308.

John Jemison and Nancy Adcock, 8 Dec. 1847, by Peter Stewart,
J.P. Page 308.

Charles D. Bush and Saleann B. Dubose, 17 Feb. 1848, by G. W.
Williams, J.P. Consent of parents, Zacheriah
Bush, and Seaborn J. Dubose. Page 310.

Wesley Bishop and Cynthia Crews, 24 Feb. 1848, by James Orr, J.P.
Page 311.

Reubin King and Georgia Ann Deshazo, 15 Feb. 1848, by James
Orr, J.P. Page 311.

Aaron Creech and Charity Creech, 27 Jan. 1848, by Jno. L.
Williams, J.P. Page 312.

Timothy W. Bludworth and Charlotte Bevel, 16 Apr. 1848, by
Appleton Haygood, M.G. Page 312.

Hardy Holmes and Amanda Grant, 4 Apr. 1848, by Daniel Cumbie,
M.G. Page 313.

Edmund West and Spicy P. Kilpatrick, 2 Dec. 1847, by Thomas J.
Head, J.P. Page 313.

J. L. C. Evans and Mrs. Martha A. Hendricks, 20 Oct. 1847, by
     Thomas J. Head, J.P.   Page 314.

James Harrod ordained at the Primitive Baptist Church at Salem,
     in Barbour County, Alabama. Recorded 18 Apr. 1848.
     Presbytery: Abner Belcher & Jesse Tomlin. Page
     314.

Patrick H. Mitchell and Garaldine Jourdan, 20 Apr. 1848, by
     J. E. Glenn. Page 315.

John Calvin Martin and Eliza M. Cannon, 3 May 1848, by Thos. H.
     Foster. Page 316.

Nicholas Smith and Nancy S. Parker, 11 Nov. 1847, by Robert
     Toler, M.G. Page 316.

Joshua Sutton and Elizabeth Hutchinson, 25 May 1848, by Edwin
     James. Page 317.

Robert W. Turner and Mary Vickers, 8 June 1848, by James Orr.
     Page 317.

Guilford Kent and Sarah Spear, 26 Apr. 1848, by Jno. L. Williams,
     J.P. Page 318.

Norman A. McIntosh and Elizabeth J. Head, 11 Apr. 1848, by Peter
     Stewart, J.P. Page 318.

Hesikiah Bass and Lucinda Beatty, 13 Apr. 1848, by Jesse Tomlin,
     M.G. Page 319.

Calvin Oglesby and Eliza Carr, 18 Feb. 1848, by Haywood Pipkin,
     J.P. Page 319.

William J. Porter and Nancy Helms, 30 Mar. 1848, by Green Malone,
     M.G. Page 320.

Isaac Gidding and Gabrella Hicks, 13 Apr. 1848, by Mathew Hall,
     J.P. Page 320.

William J. Dubose and Lucinda A. Bell, 28 Mar. 1848, by T.
     Cargile, J.P. Page 321.

Isaih Dubose and Eady Bell, 18 Mar. 1848, by T. Cargile, J.P.
     Page 321.

John Cox, Jr. and Laurey Kilpatrick, 6 July 1848, by W. N.
     Adkinson, J.P. Page 322.

Joseph Dawson and Edy M. Price, 14 July 1848, by Thos. F.
     Bloodworth, J.P. Page 322.

Richard H. Fryer and Lucinda Fenn, 25 July 1848, by Joel Sims,
     M.G. Page 323.

Solomon Butler and Catherine McKeller, 27 July 1848, by Daniel
     Campbell, J.P. Page 323.

Eli Bolton and Elizabeth Ann Carter, 7 July 1848, by Daniel
     Campbell, J.P. Page 324.

Kinion Windham and Irena Butler, 10 Aug. 1848, by Thos. F.

Bludworth, J.P. Page 324.

Andrew J. Hopkins and Miss R. M. Powell, 30 July 1848, by Jesse Tomlin, M.G. Page 325.

E. B. Cowen and Catherine McIntosh, 6 Aug. 1848, by Peter Stewart, J.P. Page 325.

Elias M. Kiels and Martha E. Sylvester, 13 Aug. 1848, by Thos. H. Foster. Page 326.

Lawson Johnston and Mary Keener, 17 Aug. 1848, by Thos. F. Bludworth, J.P. Page 327.

John Cole and Susan Jane Johnston, 24 Aug. 1848, by Thos. F. Bludworth, J.P. Page 327.

James Baxley and Rebecca Hartzogg, 17 Sept. 1848, by Jesse Tomlin, M.G. Page 327.

John N. Westbrook and Sarah A. Ketchamp, 10 Sept. 1848, by P. Bloodworth, J.P. Page 328.

John A. Gilford and Margarett Miles, 7 Sept. 1848, by P. Bludworth, J.P. Page 328.

Theophilus C. King and Elizabeth G. Harper, 16 Dec. 1847, by Andrew Cumbie, M.G. Page 329.

George M. T. Retherford and Sarah E. Martin, 11 Apr. 1848, by Andrew Cumbie, M.G. Page 329.

Steven Amons and Mary Parmer, 20 Aug. 1848, by Solomon Sikes, M.G. Page 330.

Josiah Cunningham and Elizabeth Fails, 22 Aug. 1847, by Solomon Sikes, M.G. Page 331.

Hamlin L. Wade and Elizabeth Carden, 3 Oct. 1848, by C. S. Scales, J.P. Page 331.

Jesse Canady and Mary Ann Manurva Prim, 25 July 1848, by Jno. J. Groves, M.G. Page 332.

James A. Cobb and Elizabeth Jane Weaver, 11 May 1848, by H. Pipkin, J.P. Consent of her father, Absalom Weaver. (p. 335). Page 332.

James Boyett and Rebeca Upshaw, 18 June 1848, by Haywood Pipkin, J.P. Page 333.

John B. Holston and Elizabeth Tucker, 5 Oct. 1848, by Jno. L. Williams, J.P. Page 333.

Vining Tate and Emily Fillingham, 31 Aug. 1848, by Jno. L. Williams, J.P. Page 334.

Jesse F. Johnston and Sarah Harper, 18 Oct. 1848, by Thos. F. Bludworth, J.P. Page 334.

Green B. Nolen and Alemedia Hancock, 5 Oct. 1848, by Benjamin Gardner, J.P. Page 335.

Green Miller and Elizabeth Palmer, 12 Oct. 1848, by James Orr, J.P. Page 336.

W. E. Harper and Elizabeth Watson, 24 Sept. 1848, by Thos. F. Bludworth, J.P. Page 336.

John A. Cameron and Nancy Cooper, 14 Oct. 1848, by Thomas Cargile, J.P. Page 337.

Thomas S. Smart and Cleopatria Warren, 14 Oct. 1848, by Thomas Cargile, J.P. Page 337.

E. G. Dowling and Mrs. L. S. Flournoy, 2 Nov. 1848, by A. T. Spence, J.P. Page 338.

John Davis and Lena Dowling, 10 Aug. 1848, by J. C. Weaver. Page 338.

Henry Hendrick and Mary A. Dowling, 20 June 1848, by J. C. Weaver, L.D. Page 339.

James T. Marley and Margarett McNair, 31 Oct. 1848, by Williamson Smith. Page 339.

Daniel Cumbie ordained at the Church of Christ at Sennerhill, belonging to the Salam United Baptist, Stewart Co., Ga. 23 Sept. 1844. Recorded Barbour County on 29 Nov. 1848. Presbytery: Andrew Cumbie, John Reeves & James Buyce. Page 340.

John H. McKenzie and Nancy McLeod, 16 Nov. 1848, by John L. Williams, J.P. Page 341.

John W. Faulk and Mary Ketcham, 23 Nov. 1848, by Henry Faulk, J.P. Page 341.

William Anders and Margaret Ann Grubbs, 11 Jan. 1849, by Daniel Cumbie, M.G. Page 341.

Hally Owen and Martha Powell, 25 Sept. 1848, by Robert Toler, M.G. Page 341.

Edward M. Singleton and Lerissey J. Thomas, 9 Nov. 1848, by M. W. Helms, V.D.M. Page 342.

Zapheniah Hatewell and Elizabeth Clark, 30 Nov. 1848, by Solomon Sikes. Page 342.

Benjamin W. Morrison and Tercy Segeris, 3 Aug. 1847, by Aaron Helms. Page 342.

A. C. McNab and Mrs. Pearcy Andrews, 24 Sept. 1848, by D. Cumbie, M.G. Page 342.

Seaborn H. Young and Carsey An Shedrick, 9 Nov. 1848, by M. W. Helms, V.D.M. Page 343.

William T. Watson and Sarah Bickley, 9 Nov. 1848, by H. Pipkin, J.P. Page 343.

James A. Parker and Catharine Anglin, 17 Dec. 1848, by Robert Toler, M.G. Page 343.

Elisha Stripling and Rebecca A. Hooks, 30 Nov. 1848, by Robert
        Toler, M.G.   Page 344.

Edmoniel Evans and Mary Head, executed 12 Nov. 1848.   Page 344.

Jacob Watson and Nancy Parker, 23 Nov. 1848, by Thos. P. Blud-
        worth, J.P.   Page 344.

George C. Hodges and Sarah J. Bledsoe, 21 Dec. 1848, by Jonathan
        Davis, V.D.M.   Page 344.

William Adcock and Nancy Stone, 24 Dec. 1848, by Peter Stewart,
        J.P.   Page 345.

George Atwell and Mary Jane Peterson, 11 Dec. 1848, by A. T.
        Spence, J.P.   Page 345.

Daniel G. Beverly and Nancy Beasley, 25 Jan. 1849, by O. D.
        Neily, M.G.   Page 345.

Levi Dunn and Nancy Jourdan, 14 Jan. 1849, by A. T. Spence, J.P.
        Page 345.

Garrett W. Hunt and Lucinda Bradberry, 22 Sept. 1848, by Peter
        Stewart, J.P.   Page 346.

William F. Green and Elizabeth Ellis, 25 Dec. 1848, by A. J.
        Wilson, J.P.   Page 346.

Lewis S. Spright and Esther Phillips, 9 Nov. 1848, by Peter
        Stewart, J.P.   Page 346.

Huey Foran and Weltty Wilkinson, 17 Sept. 1848, by Edwin James,
        M.G.   Page 347.

Haywood Pipkin and Eliza Cameron, 4 Jan. 1849, by Mathew Hall,
        J.P.   Page 347.

Francis W. Causey and Martha Cunningham, 24 Dec. 1848, by Andrew
        Cumbie, M.G.   Page 348.

James C. Perry and Amanda Waters, 24 Dec. 1848, by Mathew Hall,
        J.P.   Page 348.

A. D. Whittle and Mary Jane McNeal, 11 Jan. 1849, by Mathew Hall,
        J.P.   Page 349.

Wiley Eidson and Martha A. Beasley, 21 Jan. 1849, by Amos Rist,
        J.P.   Page 349.

Robert Ivy and Virginia Brown, 19 Dec. 1848, by James E. Glenn.
        Page 350.

William A. Chaney and May Holland, 29 Dec. 1848, by J. E. Glenn.
        Page 350.

F. S. C. Sumerkamp and Mary McAllister, 12 Oct. 1848, by J. E.
        Glenn.   Page 350.

Asbury W. Palmer and Mary Parker, 22 Dec. 1847, by Jno.
        Crowell, M.G.   Page 351.

Henry B. Parker and Martha Ann Bryant, 23 Dec. 1847, by J. E.

Glenn. Page 351.

Charnack A. Tharp and Mary J. E. Williamson, 26 Jan. 1849, by Henry Faulk, Jr., J.P. Page 352.

Levi Whitehurst and Mary B. Smith, 31 Jan. 1849, by James Orr, J.P. Page 352.

Daniel M. Gillis and Catherine McKenzie, 22 Feb. 1849, by James Orr, J.P. Page 353.

Abden A. Holt and Alsey A. Ivy, 8 Feb. 1849, by Benjamin Cropps. Page 353.

Lorenzo D. Brown and Elizabeth Mires, 6 Mar. 1849, by Amos Rist, J.P. Page 354.

Green Norris and Rebecca Mills, 8 Mar. 1849, by A. T. Spence, J.P. Page 354.

Mitchell Giddings and Eliza F. Seay, 10 Mar. 1849, by Thos. F. Bludworth, J.P. Page 355.

A. R. McKinley and Mary Lewis, 2 Jan. 1849, by Appleton Haygood, M.G. Page 355.

James P. Lunsford and Martha Pope, 31 Dec. 1848, by Wesley Vinson, J.P. Page 355.

Robert J. Beasley and Mrs. Sealy Baker, 1 Mar. 1849, by P. Bludworth, J.P. Page 357.

Holden Childs and Sarah Wiggins, 14 Mar. 1849, by Henry Faulk, Jr., J.P. Page 357.

H. F. McKinny and Sarah Ann McCrary, 3 Apr. 1849, by Daniel Cumbie, M.G. Page 358.

Joshua S. Callaway and Malisa A. Jordan, 17 Nov. 1847, by (illegible), V.D.M. Page 358.

Robert R. Green and Mary Ellis, 24 Nov. 1847, by A. J. Wilson, J.P. Page 359.

Edward H. Cotton and Ardelia Porter, 29 Jan. 1848, by L. C. Harrison, M.G. Page 359.

Joseph W. N. Mears ordained Deacon of the M. E. Church by Bishop Wm. Capers at Macon, Ga., 27 Dec. 1846. Recorded Barbour Co., Ala., on 11 May 1849. Page 360.

Harvey A. McRae and Lucy Shipman, 25 Mar. 1849, by M. A. Paterson, M.G. Page 361.

Thomas P. Marshall and Sarah Smith, 11 Mar. 1849, by Tompson Glenn. Page 361.

William Tucker and Mary A. Johnson, 1 Mar. 1849, by Jno. L. Williams, J.P. Page 362.

Robert A. Hightower and Elizabeth Green, 29 Apr. 1849, by A. T. Spence, J.P. Page 362.

Needham L. Pierce and Marry Ann Carroll, 21 Mar. 1849, by
Williamson Smith, J.P. Page 363.

Thomas Holleman and Amanda Davis, 3 May 1849, by James Harrod,
M.G. Page 363.

William T. Paramore and Eliza M. Fillingim, 29 Apr. 1849, by
James Harrod, M.G. Page 364.

William H. Bludworth and Mary Bevel, 6 May 1849, by A. Haygood,
M.G. Page 364.

William R. Favors and Tabitha Herring, 14 Sept. 1848, by Thos.
F. Bludworth, J.P. Page 364.

George Walker and Mrs. Mary Ann Amanda Arnold, 15 Apr. 1849, by
Wm. Sikes, M.G. Page 365.

R. G. Langston and Mrs. E. A. Renfroe, 22 Apr. 1849, by Jonathan
Davis, V.D.M. Page 365.

Erastus Bell and Elizabeth Taylor, 13 May 1849, by M. B. Wellborn,
J.P. Page 366.

Tennent Lomax and Sophia H. Shorter, 10 May 1849, by Wm. H.
McIntosh. Page 366.

A. V. McAllister and Nancy Lolless, 27 May 1849, by W. A.
Wiley, J.P. Page 366.

Jackson Blakey and Mary Ann Bowden, 31 May 1849, by W. A. Wiley,
J.P. Page 367.

Randall Faqua and Mary Hartzogg, 8 Mar. 1849, by Solomon Sikes,
M.G. Page 367.

Daniel Teel and Sarah McDowell, 8 Mar. 1849, by Solomon Sikes,
M.G. Page 368.

John Slown and Mary McDowell, 22 July 1849, by W. McCormick, J.P.
Page 368.

Joseph Thomas and Sarah Baker, 6 Aug. 1849, by James Harrod,
M.G. Page 368.

John Hargroves and Charity Herring, 4 Aug. 1849, by Wm. A.
Miles, J.P. Page 369.

William J. Addison and Lareyan Oliver, 5 Aug. 1849, by Wm. J.
Stephens, J.P. Page 369.

James Bulard and Cathrine Purves, 2 Mar. 1849, by W. N.
Adkinson, J.P. Page 369.

William Morrison and Mary Brown, 28 June 1849, by Daniel
Campbell, J.P. Page 370.

Jackson Glass and Jane A. Oliver, 26 July 1849, by A. T.
Spence, J.P. Page 370.

Bunis Phillips and Sarah Jane Sutton, 14 June 1849, by Henry
Faulk, Jr., J.P. Page 371.

Augustus L. Oliver and Ann M. Williams, 16 Jan. 1850, by Amos
Rist, J.P. Page 371.

Henry D. Clayton and Victoria Hunter, 9 Jan. 1850, by Geo.
Cushman, Episcopal Minister. Page 372.

Tergwell McNair and Masedonia Crocker, 3 Jan. 1850, by Williamson Smith, J.P. Page 372.

John D. Messer and Martha Tomlin, 30 Dec. 1849, by Williamson
Smith, J.P. Page 372.

Norl W. Turner and Margarett Stewart, 12 Dec. 1849, by Jno. L.
Williams, J.P. Page 373.

Isaac Dykes and Lida Carroll, 25 Nov. 1849, by Williamson Smith,
J.P. Page 373.

Uriah Bass and Rachael R. Price, 23 Dec. 1849, by Williamson
Smith, J.P. Page 374.

Edward Quillen and Sarah Ann E. Atkinson, 25 Dec. 1849, by
Williamson Smith, J.P. Page 374.

Stephen H. Mills and Martha Streetman, 20 Dec. 1849, by H.
Pipkin, J.P. Page 375.

James L. Hawkins and Catherine Canady, 27 Dec. 1849, by H.
Pipkin, J.P. Page 375.

Eli Thomas and Catherine Zaun, 20 Dec. 1849, by G. W. Williams,
J.P. Page 376.

Joel W. Pope and Piety Vick, 23 Dec. 1849, by Wesley Vinson,
J.P. Page 376.

William Ray and Sarah A. R. Screws, 13 Dec. 1849, by Wesley
Vinson, J.P. Page 376.

Hiram F. Lindsey and Mary Ann Nichols, 9 July 1849, by Wesley
Vinson, J.P. Page 377.

Frederick Bryan and Sarentha A. E. Davis, 4 Oct. 1849, by
Wesley Vinson, J.P. Page 377.

Peter McKnight and Jane Reynolds, 6 Dec. 1849, by James Orr,
J.P. Page 378.

James H. Oliver and Lucinda Bryant, 27 Dec. 1849, by A. T.
Spence, J.P. Page 378.

Munroe Seay and Emily Cody, 20 Sept. 1849, by Andrew Cumbie,
M.G. Page 379.

Avender Flowers and Martha Graves, 23 Dec. 1849, by Henry
Faulk, Jr., J.P. Page 379.

Henry H. Moreland and Mary D. Sutton, 20 Dec. 1849, by Henry
Faulk, Jr., J.P. Page 380.

Jacob Campbell and Mary Teal, 6 Dec. 1849, by Henry Faulk, Jr.,
J.P. Page 380.

John McKissack and Eliza Shanks, 25 Dec. 1849, by Andrew Cumbie, M.G.   Page 381.

W. B. Green and Mary Jane Cook, 3 Jan. 1850, by J. T. Hood, J.P. Page 381.

Alfred Green and Penelope M. Cook, 13 Dec. 1849, by J. T. Hood, J.P.   Page 381.

William Teal and Kessiar Smith, 15 Jan. 1850, by Solomon Sykes, M.G.   Page 382.

Daniel A. Spurlock and Mary Jones, 17 Jan. 1850, by Solomon Sikes, M.G.   Page 382.

Willis Browning and Bethena Teel, 13 Dec. 1849, by Solomon Sikes, M.G.   Page 383.

James M. Baker and Elizabeth Ann Harwell, 11 Dec. 1849, by Robert Toler, M.G.   Page 383.

William B. Bickley and Mary S. Dukes, 5 July 1849, by Andrew Cumbie, M.G.   Page 384.

Owen Broadnax and Martha Stripling, 6 Dec. 1849, by John J. Groves, minister.   Page 384.

Isaac Wells and Alley Adams, 2 Dec. 1849, by Edwin James, M.G. Page 385.

William R. Smith and Eliza Parmer, 29 Nov. 1849, by Solomon Sikes, M.G.   Page 385.

Huey (or Henry?) B. Tompson and Antoinett V. Flewellen, 30 Jan. 1849, by Jno Crowell, M.G.   Page 385.

Thomas K. Appling and Sarah J. Flake, 4 Jan. 1849, by James E. Glenn.   Page 386.

John Mrick and Jane Roling, 2 Sept. 1849, by Henry Faulk, Jr., J.P.   Page 386.

William W. Toler and Sarah Ann M. Anglin, 26 Dec. 1849, by Thos. F. Bludworth, J.P.   Page 386.

Ira A. Price and Winny Hagler, 12 Dec. 1849, by Thos. F. Bludworth, J.P.   Page 387.

John J. Cumbie ordained Baptist minister at Teman Church in Henry Co., Ga., on 17 Oct. 1841.   Recorded Barbour County, Ala., 29 Jan. 1850.   Presbytery: John P. James, James Cleveland, Eph. Strickland, James Cumbie and Spencer Harvey.   Page 387.

William S. Nolan and Ruthy Jane Bullock, 15 Jan. 1850, by Edwin James, M.G.   Page 388.

Walter L. B. R. Parker and Ann McRae, 7 Feb. 1850, by Thompson Glenn.   Page 388.

William D. Cooper and Matilda Parmer, 17 Jan. 1850, by G. W. Williams, J.P.   Page 389.

John Watson and Mary R. Bush, 10 Jan. 1850, by G. W. Williams, J.P. Page 389.

Thomas J. Faison and Sarah Jane Bryan, 20 Dec. 1849, by Elder W. Lee. Page 390.

Munroe Stafford and Elenor Richards, 1 Feb. 1850, by James Orr, J.P. Page 390.

John W. Clark and Mary E. Kiels, 29 Jan. 1850, by E. R. Ware. Page 391.

A. S. Robinson and Martha Jane McNeil, 17 Jan. 1850, by W. B. Wellborn, J.P. Page 391.

Michael W. Blair and Martha Hargroves, 10 Jan. 1850, by Jesse Tomlin, M.G. Page 392.

W. L. Loveless and Nancy C. Warren, 4 Nov. 1849, by W. M. Miles, J.P. Page 392.

1849 records from Marriage Book IV.

Jacob Parmer and Adeline Baker, 4 Oct. 1849, by Solomon Sikes, M.G. Page 1.

John McMichael and Narcessa Neice, 6 Sept. 1849, by Thos. F. Bludworth, J.P. Page 1.

Francis M. Hagler and Martha Brady, 11 Oct. 1849, by Thos. F. Bludworth, J.P. Page 1.

Absolam T. Dawkins and Mrs. Mary A. C. Moore, 18 Oct. 1849, by Jno. L. Williams, J.P. Page 1.

Cornelius Shipes and Mary A. M. Brewer, 17 Oct. 1849, by Wm. Luker, M.G. Page 2.

Redding Baxley and Rachael McCarrell, 16 Oct. 1849, by Williamson Smith, J.P. Page 2.

L. D. Chambers and Mary Kinims, 11 Oct. 1849, by Williamson Smith, J.P. Page 2.

James L. Stewart and Miss L. J. Wise, 10 Oct. 1849, by J. W. Holston, M.G. Page 2.

John Creel and Mary Sikes, 15 Feb. 1849, by Z. Wood, J.P. Page 2.

Ellison Baker and Mary Cooper, 27 Sept. 1849, by James Harrod, M.G. Page 3.

James J. Baker and Nancy Williamson, 8 Sept. 1849, by G. W. Williams, J.P. Page 3.

Hampton Casey and Hepsey A. B. Price, 3 June 1849, by Thos. F. Bludworth, J.P. Page 3.

William McLeod and Francis E. Birdsong, 17 June 1849, by L. C. Harrison, M.G. Page 3.

John W. Herring and Catherine Butler, 23 Sept. 1849, by Wm. A.

Miles, J.P. Page 4.

William Powell and Elizabeth McMurray, 12 Sept. 1849, by Joel
        Sims, M.G. Page 4.

John Bently and Fanny Thomas, 25 July 1849, by Aaron Helms.
        Page 4.

John Bently, Jr., and Catherine Walker, 17 June 1849, by Aaron
        Helms. Page 4.

Moses E. Bush and Elizabeth J. Grubs, 15 Aug. 1849, by G. W.
        Williams, J.P. Page 5.

James W. Hartzogg and Martha A. J. Warr, 2 July 1849, by
        Williamson Smith, J.P.   Consent of his mother,
        Sealy Mitchell and her father, John Warr. Page 5.

Jonathan P. Wilkinson and Nancy A. A. Purvis, 4 Nov. 1849, by
        Uriah M. Pelham, M.G. Page 5.

Green Stephens and Margarett McRae, 19 Aug. 1849, by Tompson
        Glenn. Page 6.

James Volentine and Hester Ann Taylor, 23 Mar. 1849, by W. N.
        Atkinson, J.P. Page 6.

Samuel W. South and Sany Riley, 7 Sept. 1848, by W. N. Atkinson,
        J.P. Page 6.

Eleson DuBose and Lucinda Basset, 29 Apr. 1849, by Edwin James,
        minister. Page 6.

William Spurlock and Sarah Bird, 2 Aug. 1849, by Elijah Ray,
        J.P. Page 7.

Perry H. Jones and Martha Shipes, 13 Apr. 1849, by Aaron Helms.
        Page 7.

Colin Gardner and Mrs. Jane Hemphill, 20 June 1849, by W. H.
        McIntosh. Page 7.

Jackson Anderson and Fanny Bryan, 2 Jan. 1849, by Aaron Helms.
        Page 7.

Lewis L. Cato and Martha Jane Richardson, 28 June 1849, by
        Thos. H. D. Sealy, M.G. Page 8.

William McNair and Mary Saunders, 6 Nov. 1849, by P. Bludworth,
        J.P. Page 9.

John M. Saunders and Susan Sims, 9 Dec. 1849, by P. Bludworth,
        J.P. Page 9.

George W. Coleman and Lucy Greenwood, 5 Dec. 1849, by A. N.
        Worthy, M.G. Page 9.

B. F. Beverly and Elizabeth Honeman, 4 Dec. 1849, by Harris
        Sterry, M.G. Page 10.

Jerrod Sanders Dennard ordained in the Perry Baptist Church in
        Houston Co., Ga., on 1 Feb. 1849. Recorded
        Barbour County 24 Apr. 1850. Adam T. Holmes,

Perry Baptist Church. J. H. Campbell, Richland Church, Twiggs County, Georgia. Page 12.

Asa Wilkinson licensed to preach at a meeting held at Primitive Baptist Church, Choctawhatchee, in Barbour Co., Ala. on 21 Aug. 1847. Recorded 30 Apr. 1850. Jesse Tomlin & Gabrul Purswell. Page 13.

Daniel McLeod and Pamelia McGill, 31 Oct. 1848, by J. W. Holston, M.G. Page 13.

John A. Watson and Pricilo Harrall, 4 Dec. 1849, by John G. Cowan, M.G. Page 20.

Nathan O. Glover and Elizabeth Fort, 2 Apr. 1846, by John Cowan, M.G. Page 25.

Samuel DeLoach and Catherine Gilchrist, 7 Mar. 1849, by M. Gilchrist, J.P. Page 26.

L. F. Johnston and Martha F. Bethune, 6 Dec. 1849, by S. Armstrong. Page 27.

Andrew J. Cleman and Virlinda Caton, 15 Nov. 1849, by Benjamin Cropp. Page 58.

Augustus W. Barnett and Celestia B. Treutlin, 18 Dec. 1849, by J. E. Glenn, L.M. Page 58.

William H. McIntosh ordained in the Baptist faith on the 3rd Lord's Day 1836, at South Newport, in McIntosh County, Georgia. Recorded Barbour County, Ala., 12 Feb. 1853. Presbytery: Samuel L. Law, James McDonald & Josiah S. Law. Page 87.

John D. Collins ordained 5 Nov. 1842 at the Baptist Church at Antioch, Jones County, Georgia. Recorded Barbour County, Ala., 17 Feb. 1853. Luke Newell, Mod.; Jas. P. Lowe, Clk.

HERE ENDS BOOK IV

1850 MARRIAGES FROM MARRIAGE BOOK I

Augustus L. Oliver and Ann M. Williams, 16 Jan. 1850, by Amos Rist, J.P. Page 371.

Henry D. Clayton and Victoria Hunter, 9 Jan. 1850, by Geo. Cushman, Episcopal minister. Page 372.

Targwell McNair and Masedonia Crocker, 3 Jan. 1850, by Williamson Smith, J.P. Page 372.

W. B. Green and Mary Jane Cook, 3 Jan. 1850, by J. T. Hood, J.P. Page 381.

William Teal and Kessiar Smith, 15 Jan. 1850, by Soln. Sikes, M.G. Page 382.

Daniel A. Spurlock and Mary Jones, 17 Jan. 1850, by Soln. Sikes, M.G. Page 382.

William S. Nolan and Ruthy Jane Bullock, 15 Jan. 1850, by Edwin
    James, M.G. Page 382.

Walter L. B. R. Parker and Ann McRae, 7 Feb. 1850, by Thompson
    Glenn. Page 388.

William D. Cooper and Matilda Parmer, 17 Jan. 1850, by G. W.
    Williams, J.P. Page 389.

Munroe Stafford and Elenor Richards, 1 Feb. 1850, by James
    Orr, J.P. Page 390.

John W. Clark and Mary E. Kiels, 29 Jan. 1850, by E. R. Ware.
    Page 391.

A. S. Robinson and Martha Jane McNeil, 17 Jan. 1850, by W. S.
    Wellborn, J.P. Page 391.

Michael W. Blair and Martha Hargroves, 10 Jan. 1850, by Jesse
    Tomlin, M.G. Page 392.

1850 Marriages cont'd.

John K. Hollingsworth and Mary Parker, 21 Feb. 1850, by Thos. F.
    Bloodworth, J.P. Page 3.

George W. Atwell and Sarah Peterson, 7 Feb. 1850, by A. T.
    Spence, J.P. Page 6.

Stephen Olin Capers ordained in the M. E. Church on 20 Jan. 1850
    at Columbus, Mi. Bishop Wm. Capers. Recorded
    Barbour County 12 Mar. 1850. Page 8.

Thomas F. Pugh and Nancy McSwain, 26 Feb. 1850, by E. Ward.
    Page 9.

William Dykes and Jane Walker, 10 Mar. 1850, by J. A. Jones, J.P.
    Page 9.

Levi Glass and Elizabeth Creech, 3 Mar. 1850, by James Orr, J.P.
    Page 10.

Abner L. Broach and Catherine Rouse, 7 Mar. 1850, by Appleton
    Haygood, M.G. Page 10.

Young Smith and Sarah McLeod, 3 Mar. 1850, by Jno. L. Williams,
    J.P. Page 10.

Gilford Kent and Susan Brown, 21 Feb. 1850, by Jno. L. Williams,
    J.P. Page 10.

Daniel J. Sims and Mary Ann Butler, 14 Mar. 1850, by J. A.
    Jones, J.P. Consent of his father, Avey Sims,
    and her father, Samuel Butler, for them to inter-
    marry. Page 11.

Edward R. Ware ordained at Prattville on 24 Oct. 1849 to the
    Presbyterian Church. Recorded 6 Apr. 1850.
    Page 11.

Lewis Lindsey and Elizabeth Flinn, 3 Apr. 1850, by Franklin E.

Baker, J.P. Page 12.

Charles Picket and Charity P. Norton, 25 Apr. 1850, by Jno. C. Carter, M.G. Page 13.

J. W. Huey and Amanda Grubs, 25 Apr. 1850, by Henry Faulk, J.P. Page 13.

Cary F. Windham and Sophia Skipper, 18 Apr. 1850, by Harris Sterry, M.G. Page 13.

John Lewis and Elizabeth D. Hitchcock, 27 Apr. 1850, by H. M. Tompkins, J.P. Page 14.

Joshua Hand and Sarah Carter, 21 Mar. 1850, by Daniel Campbell, J.P. Page 14.

Josiah Bass and Alsey Hutson, 7 Apr. 1850, by William Smith. Page 14.

William J. Barrow and Ann H. Denson, 12 Feb. 1850, by Wesley Vinson, J.P. Page 14.

John C. Beasley and Barbary Beasley, 12 May 1850, by Wm. Hinson, J.P. Page 14.

James M. Hughs and Martha J. Johnson, 16 May 1850, by Dow. Perry, M.G. Page 15.

William King and Sarah Cabaness, 19 May 1850, by M. B. Wellborn, J.P. Page 15.

Dennis Nolin and Martha E. J. Dubose, 2 June 1850, by Edwin James, M.G. Page 15.

William Barnum and Sarah Taylor, 26 Mar. 1850, by Elijah Ray, J.P. Page 15.

Ransom D. Singleton and Caroline Neice, 4 June 1850, by Wm. Hinson, J.P. Page 16.

William Loveless and Mrs. Nancy Warren, 9 June 1850, by Joel Sims, M.G. Page 16.

James A. Gillinwater and Miss J. A. Forte, 30 May 1850, by M. B. Wellborn, J.P. Page 16.

John Thompson and Martha Thorn, 16 May 1850, by Henry Faulk, Jr., J.P. Page 16.

Mark W. Faulk and Marinah Joiner, 6 June 1850, by Henry Faulk, Jr., J.P. Page 17.

Samuel Slaughter and Jane Patterson, 23 June 1850, by A. T. Spence, J.P. Page 17.

J. L. Roberts and Sarah Oliver, 26 June 1850, by Edward R. Ware. Page 17.

William A. Nolin and Becky Ann Glass, 30 June 1850, by Edwin James, M.G. Page 17.

Asa Beasley and Sarah A. E. Anglin, 8 July 1850, by H. M.

Tompkins, J.P.   Page 18.

Nelson Stuart and Jane Evans, 13 June 1850, by Jno. Reid, J.P.
          Page 18.

Bryant Bass and Shelomath E. Tye, 18 July 1850, by G. W.
          Carter, M.G.   Page 18.

Daniel F. Beasley and Miss C. J. Herring, 30 July 1850, by Wm.
          Hinson, J.P.   Page 18.

T. E. Warren and Sophornia Loveless, 1 Aug. 1850, by Wm. Hinson,
          J.P.   Page 19.

Isac R. W. Lewis and Martha A. Creel, 6 Aug. 1850, by W. P.
          Sanders, J.P.   Page 19.

Samuel Feagin and Julia T. Murel, 28 Feb. 1850, by J. J.
          Dickinson, M.G.   Page 19.

Daniel C. McEachern and Sarah Lee, 18 July 1850, by L. L.
          Pierce, J.P.   Page 19.

Thomas Johnson and Bethenia Cost, 6 Aug. 1850, by J. P. Jones,
          J.P.   Page 19.

Mathew Jones and Isabel McDonald, 9 May 1850, by P. Bludworth,
          J.P.   Page 20.

C. C. McRae and Nancy A. Campbell, 8 Aug. 1850, by P. Bloodworth,
          J.P.   Page 20.

Sion Hill and Sarah Wilks, 3 June 1850, by P. Bludworth, J.P.
          Page 20.

James Cox and Miss J. A. Gunnels, 6 July 1850, by P. Bludworth,
          J.P.   Page 20.

Thomas Tilett and Mary Stephenson, 11 Aug. 1850, by Wm. Hinson,
          J.P.   Page 21.

John M. Hudspeth and Mary A. Cole, 12 Oct. 1850, by Joel Sims,
          M.G.   Page 21.

W. W. Gomillion and Frances Rigdon, 15 Oct. 1850, by Wm.
          Galaway, M.G.   Page 21.

Middleton Brooks ordained at Mount Zion Church, Barbour County,
          on 14 Apr. 1849.   Recorded 3 Jan. 1851.   Page 21.

Andrew J. Gomillion and Mary A. Rigdon, 11 Dec. 1850, by Middle-
          ton Brooks.   Page 22.

J. P. Swinny and Elizabeth Streeter, 9 Jan. 1851, by Peter
          Stewart, J.P.   Page 22.

Alexander Blanton and Susan Petty, issued 22 Jan. 1851, executed,
          M. B. Wellborn, J.P.   Page 22.

N. P. Banks and Frances A. Jernigan, 16 Jan. 1851, by G. W.
          Carter, M.G.   Page 22.

Henry Carroll and Louisa M. McNair, 23 Jan. 1851, by Lovard L.

43

Pierce, J.P. Page 22.

Wesley T. Mayo and Martha Burgess, 6 Jan. 1851, by L.L. Pierce, J.P. Page 23.

B. E. G. Parmer and Maryann Holly, 23 Jan. 1851, by Joel Sims, M.G. Page 23.

William A. Coleman and Sarah E. West, 28 Nov. 1850, by H. Pipkin, J.P. Page 23.

M. D. L. Mayo and Catherine Chaney, 29 Dec. 1850, by Wm. Hinson, J.P. Page 23.

Nolin Stricklin and Emeline Crabtree, 2 Jan. 1851, by J. T. Cole, J.P. Page 23.

John Mingo and Susan Sutton, 5 Dec. 1850, by John Reed, J.P. Page 23.

William Bishop and Rebecca S. Warren, 12 Dec. 1850, by H. M. Tompkins, J.P. Page 24.

William Usery and Mary Morrison, 7 July 1850, by Jno. W. Norton. Page 24.

Elenzar Larkins and Nancy M. Bowen, 17 Oct. 1850, by Jno. G. Cowan, M.G. Page 24.

A. T. Glenn and Martha F. Peak, 21 Nov. 1850, by S. Olin Capers, M.G. Page 24.

Richard Morris and Elizabeth J. Cargill, 26 Dec. 1850, by W. H. McIntosh. Page 24.

William Winslet and Catherine Miller, 26 Dec. 1850, by Soln. Sikes, D.D. Page 25.

William H. Fort and Sarah Selah, 19 Dec. 1850, by W. B. Wellborn, J.P. Page 25.

Isac Stricklin and Naroesa Cowan, 8 Oct. 1850, by John G. Cowan, M.G. Page 25.

Needham Lee, Sr. and Sarah Sloan, 16 Oct. 1850, by H. Sterns, M.G. Page 25.

Hugh Gillis and Jane Norton, 16 May 1850, by H. F. Reaves, J.P. Page 25.

George Palmer and Nancy Dubose, 20 Oct. 1850, by H. F. Reaves, J.P. Page 26.

William Kelly and Sarah Baxly, 17 Oct. 1850, by Wm. Smith, J.P. Page 26.

Marion M. Watson and Patience Johnson, 12 Sept. 1850, by H. F. Reaves, J.P. Page 26.

David S. Easterling and Sealy Kelly, 18 Sept. 1850, by P. Bludworth, J.P. Page 26.

Allen Teal and Mary Mooneham, 12 Sept. 1850, by Daniel Campbell,

Emanuel Heath and Elizabeth Rogers, 9 Dec. 1850, executed.
Page 27.

Gillis Jackson and Eliza Grant, 3 Nov. 1850, by Henry Faulk, Jr.,
J.P.   Page 27.

Fra(n)cis W. Parrish and Martha Daul, 14 Nov. 1850, by Daniel
Campbell, J.P.   Page 27.

Jerimreah Peddy and Jane Craigg, 18 Sept. 1850, by Wesley
Vinson, J.P.   Page 27.

B. R. Hood and Sarah L. Johnston, 12 Sept. 1850; by Wm. Gallaway,
M.G.   Page 28.

William Taylor and Sintha Lawless, 22 Sept. 1850, by Peter
Stewart, J.P.   Page 28.

James McGinnis and Nancy Butts, 25 Aug. 1850, by L. L. Pierce,
J.P.   Page 28.

Thomas Whittsett and Elvira M. Daniel, 3 Oct. 1850, by Wm.
Hinson, J.P.   Page 28.

T. T. Rogers and Lusiann Blake, 25 Aug. 1850, by Franklin E.
Baker, J.P.   Page 28.

Cornelious Clemens and Ruthy Whitsett, 24 Oct. 1850, by G. W.
Williams, J.P.   Page 28.

Godfrey Lee and Miss S. A. A. McNair, 1 Aug. 1850, by Lovard L.
Pierce, J.P.   Page 29.

William Flemming and Elisa Carrol, 11 July 1850, by William
Smith, J.P.   Page 29.

Leroy Thomas and Sarah Appling, 3 Nov. 1850, by J. A. Jones, J.P.
Consent of his father, Leroy Thomas, and her
father, Thomas Appling, for them to intermarry.
Page 29.

Allen Hutto and Sarah A. Bennet, 14 Oct. 1850, by Wm. Hinson,
J.P.   Page 29.

Hiram Danby and Maryan Daner, 23 Dec. 1850, by Henry Faulk, Jr.,
J.P.   Consent of her father, Thomas M. Daner.
Page 30.

R. C. Chisolm and Martha Taylor, 29 Sept. 1850, by Peter Stewart,
J.P.   Page 30.

Easley Lott and Elizabeth Cowertly, 12 May 1850, by H. Pipkin,
J.P.   Page 30.

William Camp and Nancy Ramsey, 11 Nov. 1850, by Daniel Cambel,
J.P.   Page 30.

Randolph W. Bowen and Charlott Clark, 3 Apr. 1851, by H. F.
Reaves, J.P.   Page 30.

Thomas Harlin and Lucy A. Cumbie, 5 Jan. 1851, by J. J. Cumbie,

M.G.   Page 31.

Fair Dennis and Mary Bullock, 23 Dec. 1850, by H. F. Reaves,
          J.P.   Page 31.

C. P. Long and Amanda Maddox, 20 Apr. 1851, by Malcom Gilchrist,
          J.P.   Page 31.

William Jackson and Emeline Singleton, 22 Dec. 1850, by Wm.
          Smith, J.P.   Page 31.

E. G. Lott and Nancy Butts, 2 Mar. 1851, by Gilbert McEachern,
          J.P.   Page 31.

Lewis Stevens and Isebella S. Berry, 2 Mar. 1851, by Gilbert
          McEachern, J.P.   Page 31.

John W. Martin and Elizabeth Harrison, 23 Mar. 1851, by Gilbert
          McEachern, J.P.   Page 32.

Samuel D. Irwin and Julia A. Cargill, 29 Jan. 1851, by W.
          Mathew, M.G.   Page 32.

Joseph C. Patterson and Cliff Glass, 12 Mar. 1851, by Alpheus
          Baker, J.P.   Page 32.

Henry Giles and Jane Hall, 12 Jan. 1851, by G. W. Powell, M.G.
          Page 32.

Eli L. Griffin and Martha Ann Posy, 28 Nov. 1850, by Andrew
          Cumbie, M.G.   Page 32.

Robert Worthington and Mary E. Peak, 25 Oct. 1850, by Andrew
          Cumbie, M.G.   Page 33.

John B. Ethridge and Alletta Melton, 23 Jan. 1851, by R. E.
          Brown, M.G.   Page 33.

John Price and Martha Wells, 7 Jan. 1851, by Edwin James, M.G.
          Page 33.

John Pipkins and Percelo J. Hatcher, 13 Mar. 1851, by Z. Wood,
          J.P.   Page 33.

Alphous Baker and Louise L. Garvin, 7 Jan. 1851, by W. H.
          McIntosh.   Page 33.

William Dennis and Emela Chapman, 8 Jan. 1851, by Joel Sims,
          M.G.   Page 33.

Daniel L. Stewart and Miss E. F. Smith, 6 Feb. 1851, by L. S.
          Glenn.   Page 34.

Bery Hill and Martha Albrittan, 28 Feb. 1851, by J. T. Cole,
          J.P.   Page 34.

Joel D. Warren and Hanah M. Lampley, 4 Mar. 1851, by P.
          Bludworth, J.P.   Page 34.

Robert Calloway and Martha Pickett, 5 Nov. 1850, by J. J.
          Dickson, M.G.   Page 34.

Henson K. Paul and Rebecca Jane Watson, 21 Nov. 1851, by J. J.

Dickson, M.G.   Page 34.

George Renolds and Ann Slack, 11 May 1851, by Thompson Glenn,
        minister.   Page 35.

Paul H. Deshazo and Sarah Ginnrights, 2 Apr. 1851, by H. G.
        Reaves, J.P.   Page 35.

D. G. Campbell and Miss A. J. Wood, 18 Mar. 1851, by Z. Wood,
        J.P.   Page 35.

Stephen Chance and Nancy E. Lewis, 8 May 1851, by F. E. Baker,
        J.P.   Page 35.

James W. Cameron and Epsey Ann Taylor, 2 Jan. 1851, by H. F.
        Reaves, J.P.   Page 35.

Angus McInnis and Unity Ellis, 20 May 1851, by W. B. Wellborn,
        J.P.   Page 36.

Mark Elmore and Elizabeth Flemins, 9 May 1851, by Edwin James,
        M.G.   Page 36.

Abner A. Baleigh and Harret Lewis, 10 June 1851, by Wm. H.
        McIntosh, Baptist minister.   Page 36.

John G. Barr and Jane Silas, 1 June 1851, by F. E. Baker, J.P.
        Page 36.

Charles A. Dreggars and Sarah A. Simmons, 21 June 1851, by Wm.
        Hinson, J.P.   Page 36.

Franklin Cobb and Nancy Faison, 7 May 1851, by Peter Stewart,
        J.P.   Page 37.

George W. Hall and Katharine S. Wellborn, 23 Mar. 1851, by
        G. W. Purnell, M.G.   Page 37.

Samuel McBride and Mary Morrise, 2 June 1850, by Green Malone,
        M.G.   Page 37.

B. D. Loveless ordained at Senter Ridge Baptist Church, Barbour
        County, 30 Aug. 1851.   Presbytery: Joel Sims,
        Wm. G. Collier & Middleton Brooks.   Page 37.

T. T. Vickers made Bishop at Bethel Church, Barbour Co., on 10
        Feb. 1850.   Presbytery: John Kelly & Moses
        Pridgeon.   Recorded 23 Oct. 1851.   Page 38.

David Kennedy and Harret Shelby, 25 May 1851, by J. J. Cumbie,
        M.G.   Page 38.

John T. Smith and Cyntha E. Miller, 2 Sept. 1851, by Soln.
        Sikes, D.D.   Page 38.

George M. T. Caton and Mary Seay, 16 Oct. 1851, by J. J.
        Dickson, M.G.   Page 38.

Alexr. M. Johnson and Sarah Brown, 2 Oct. 1851, by Wm. Galaway,
        M.G.   Page 38.

John R. Lany and Emeline Cooper, 18 Sept. 1851, by James Harrod,
        M.G.   Page 39.

William Sharp and Susan Neice, 12 Oct. 1851, by B. Williams,
J.P. Page 39.

James H. Barrow and Sarah A. Bryant, 9 Oct. 1851, by John Reed,
J.P. Page 39.

Daniel McGilvary and Harriett Morley, 14 Aug. 1851, by Lovard
L. Pierce, J.P. Page 39.

Silas M. Wilks and Sarah Ann Stewart, 30 July 1851, by H. G.
Reaves, J.P. Page 39.

John Vickers and Amanda M. Martin, 15 Oct. 1851, by Z. Wood,
J.P. Page 39.

Abner Belcher and Emeline Grubs, 3 July 1851, by H. G. Reaves,
J.P. Page 40.

B. C. Riley and Elizabeth A. Cole, 22 June 1851, by Wm.
Galaway, M.G. Page 40.

Amos Arrington and Sarah C. Cole, 22 May 1851, by Wm. Galaway,
M.G. Page 40.

Lewis A. Jones and Martha Watson, 24 Aug. 1851, by A. T.
Spence, J.P. Page 40.

Aaron Rochester and Nancy Hutson, 31 July 1851, by A. T. Spence,
J.P. Page 40.

Alfred Childs and Amanda Barrow, 13 Sept. 1851, by H. M.
Tompkins, J.P. Page 41.

John D. McIntosh and Nancy A.K. Martin, 15 June 1851, by Malcom
Gilchrist, J.P. Page 41.

Joseph Thigpen ordained in the Primitive Baptist Church,
Barbour County, on 28 June 1851. Presbytery:
Robert Toler, Wm. Galaway, J. J. Dickson and James
Harrod. Page 41.

H. H. Hodges and Eliza C. Lowman, 24 July 1851, by John C.
Carter, M.G. Page 41.

Zacheriah Bush and Elizabeth Walls, 3 Sept. 1851, by B.
Williams, J.P. Page 41.

James Chancy and Jennita Pate, 3 July 1851, by Henry Faulk, Jr.,
J.P. Page 42.

William Lee and Mary Young, 7 Aug. 1851, by Daniel Cumbie, M.G.
Page 42.

J. F. Hatcher and Harriet A. McNeel, 12 Oct. 1851, by T. S.
Glenn, M.G. Page 42.

Thomas J. Shepard and Sarah Bledsoe, 16 Sept. 1851, by W. B.
Wellborn, J.P. Page 42.

James Taylor and Eliza Dorman, 4 June 1851, by P. Bludworth,
J.P. Page 42.

Abram Brown and Sally Segars, 24 Aug. 1851, by Aaron Helms.

Page 42.

Alfred Casey and Mary F. Jordan, 10 July 1851, by E. U. Wilks, J.P. Page 43.

U. L. Creech and Hany A. Lindsey, 28 Aug. 1851, by F. E. Baker, J.P. Page 43.

James Day and Vinny Avant, 30 July 1851, by L. L. Pierce, J.P. Page 43.

William C. McLoud and Eliza McDowell, 8 May 1851, by P. Bludworth, J.P. Page 43.

Richard R. Rushing ordained at Bethlehem Baptist Church in Barbour County on 30 Dec. 1851. Recorded 17 Jan. 1852. Page 44.

Thomas R. B. Vickers recorded his credentials as a Minister of the Gospel on 17 Jan. 1852. Page 44.

William Williamson and Fatha Ann Bryan, 8 Jan. 1852, by M. Gilchrist, J.P. Page 44.

Andrew Womble and Caroline Owens, 29 Feb. 1852, by W. B. Wellborn, J.P. Page 45.

George W. Hardwick and Jane Croly, 27 Jan. 1852, by Wm. Gallaway, M.G. Page 45.

John Tew and Fanny T. Morten (Martin?), 5 Oct. 1851, by Malcolm Matheson, J.P. Page 45.

Z. Benefield and Miss E. Hartzog, 1 Oct. 1851, by W. A. Adkinson, J.P. Page 45.

Hampton Ryan and Susannah Baker, 4 Feb. 1852, by H. F. Reaves, J.P. Page 45.

Joseph Peacock and Martha Ann Myers, 23 Dec. 1851, by H. F. Reaves, J.P. Page 46.

Solomon Hart and Elizabeth Nichols, 10 Dec. 1851, by H. F. Reaves, J.P. Page 46.

Chinchleen Whittle and Emeline E. Camber, 8 Feb. 1852, by Joel Simms, M.G. Page 46.

Henry Sims and Jane V. Craps, 9 Oct. 1851, by Andrew Cumbie, M.G. Page 46.

Thomas Davis and Nancy Posy, 11 Dec. 1851, by A. Cumbie, M.G. Page 46.

John C. Corley and Ariadna Hampton, 4 Sept. 1851, by A. Cumbie, M.G. Page 47.

John W. Bledsoe and Lellis A. Turk, 1 Nov. 1851, by Andrew Cumbie, M.G. Page 47.

Ichabod Stuckley and Elizabeth Willis, 3 Dec. 1851, by A. Cumbie, M.G. Page 47.

John N. McRae and Catherine McRae, 25 Jan. 1852, by D. Campbell, J.P. Page 47.

John Owens and Martha A. Atwell, 15 Jan. 1852, by F. E. Baker, J.P. Page 47.

B. F. Davis and Miss F. A. McCrary, 15 Jan. 1852, by A. T. Spence, J.P. Page 48.

William J. Telleres and Martha Ann Menshaw, 1 Jan. 1852, by Henry Faulk, Jr., J.P. Page 48.

Gregory Anderson and Lewser Menshaw, 28 Dec. 1851, by Elisha Williams, minister. Page 48.

John Cortney and Margaret Ramsey, 11 Jan. 1852, by Daniel Campbell, J.P. Page 48.

Mathew Fenn and Miss M. C. Weston, 11 Jan. 1852, by Wm. R. Cowen, Judge of Probate. Page 48.

Henry Smith and Mary Miller, 4 Jan. 1852, by Solomon Sikes, D.D. Page 49.

Thomas V. Tate and Elizabeth Bailey, 8 Jan. 1852, by James Harrod, M.G. Page 49.

George Keachey and Isabella McEachern, 1 Jan. 1852, by A. M. Patterson, M.G. Page 49.

C. D. Hightower and C. D. Jane Bush, 6 Jan. 1852, by A. T. Spence, J.P. Page 49.

David Davis and Sarah Williams, 24 Dec. 1851, by G. W. Williams, J.P. Consent of her guardian, J. E. Crews, for her to intermarry. Page 50.

Thomas R. Adams and Elizabeth McIntosh, 21 Dec. 1851, by Peter Stewart, J.P. Page 50.

James R. Lasiter and Louise E. Duke, 1 Jan. 1852, by James Harrod, M.G. Page 50.

John A. Presson and Susan Dilleshaw, 25 Dec. 1851, by David Campbell, J.P. Page 50.

William D. Kinard and Clementina Alexander, 23 Dec. 1851, by F. E. Baker, J.P. Page 50.

James Bates and Sarah J. Cox, 27 Nov. 1851, by Middleton Brooks. Page 51.

John Wynn and Eveline Gunnels, 18 Dec. 1851, by Middleton Brooks. Page 51.

William Warlick and Martha A. K. McLendon, 23 Dec. 1851, by Wesley Vinson, J.P. Page 51.

Jackson Avsett and Mary E. Sanford, 18 Dec. 1851, by W. Vinson, J.P. Page 51.

Robert Sanford and Frances Craigg, 20 Nov. 1851, by W. Vinson, J.P. Page 51.

John Peak and Rebecca Craigg, 2 Nov. 1851, by Wesley Vinson,
J.P.   Page 52.

James Driggars and Mrs. Mary Jackson, 17 Jan. 1851, executed.
Page 52.

Reding B. McDonald and Caroline M. J. Ruse, 28 Nov. 1850, by
Wesley Vinson, J.P.   Page 52.

John D. Duffell and Mary Ann Warlick, 21 Feb. 1851, by Wesley
Vinson, J.P.   Page 52.

James G. Rogers and Susannah Stephenson, 19 Dec. 1850, by
Wesley Vinson, J.P.   Page 52.

John McMichael and Eley Ann Giddings, 28 Dec. 1851, by W. R.
Cowen, Judge of Probate.   Page 53.

Lewis D. Ward and Julia Ann Warren, 21 Dec. 1851, by B. D.
Loveless, M.G.   Page 53.

Maynard D. Stobel and Caroline L. Bullock, 16 Dec. 1851, by John
Blackmon, L.L.D.   Page 53.

Felix Hight and Dellila Jerry, 23 Nov. 1851, by G. W. Carter,
M.G.   Page 53.

S. D. Staleham and Elizabeth Lewis, 15 Nov. 1851, by L. C.
Harrison, M.G.   Page 53.

Harrison Birdsong and Martha M. Sims, 18 Nov. 1851, by G. W.
Williams, J.P.   Page 54.

George W. Cotton and Missouri F. Daniel, 19 Nov. 1851, by W. H.
McIntosh, M.G.   Page 54.

Bassianus Nichols and Roberta Roberts, 20 Nov. 1851, by W. H.
McIntosh, M.G.   Page 54.

Moses Sinquefield and Mrs. Amanda Beckham, 20 Nov. 1851, by
W. H. McIntosh.   Page 54.

Larkin W. Burleson and Elizabeth Burleson, 20 Nov. 1850, by
F. E. Baker, J.P.   Page 54.

D. H. L. Bishop and Caroline Streeter, 3 Oct. 1851, by Malcom
Gilchrist, J.P.   Page 55.

B. F. Bowen and Elvira F. Glenn, 3 June 1851, by G. M. Carter,
M.G.   Page 55.

R. H. Dawkins and Mary Richards, 4 Nov. 1851, by J. W. Corbitt,
S.D.   Page 55.

Hezekiah Huggins and Necy Menshaw, 7 Sept. 1851, by Elisha
Williams, M.G.   Page 55.

A. P. Avant and Emily Dilleshaw, 2 July 1851, by E. U. Wilks,
J.P.   Page 55.

A. J. Martin and Nancy A. Bevil, 30 Oct. 1851, by F. E. Baker,
J.P.   Page 55.

Asa Blakey and Margaret C. Blakey, 10 Mar. 1852, by B. Williams, J.P. Page 56.

John Walker and Sarah Tate, 19 Feb. 1852, by Jas. Harrod, M.G. Page 56.

A. J. Johnson and Leonora L. Harrison, 29 Oct. 1851, by Jno. Reid, J.P. Consent of her mother, Mary A. McDonald, for her daughter Leonora to intermarry. Page 56.

T. P. C. Phillips and Hulday Sutton, 7 Mar. 1851, by Elder William Lee. Page 56.

Benjamin A. Covington and Sarah J. Langford, 13 Nov. 1851, by John Crowell, M.G. Page 57.

William Bush and Rebecca J. Wood, 27 May 1851, by J. A. Clement, M.G. Page 57.

John Hagler and Emeline Martin, 18 Mar. 1852, by F. E. Baker, J.P. Page 57.

James Ticner and Ann E. Cropps, 18 July 1850, by George S. Cushman. Page 57.

Marshall Vann and Nancy Jane Hardwick, 24 Dec. 1850, by J. R. W. Brown. Page 57.

A. B. Seals and Mary Frances Bradley, 8 July 1851, by J. A. Clements, M.G. Page 58.

John O. Lamar and Martha Ann E. Davis, 18 Feb. 1850, by Geo. W. Carter, M.G. Page 58.

Thomas J. Morman and Sarah Jane Wimberly, 25 Sept. 1851, by Jno. Quattlebum, J.P. Page 58.

James A. Lewis and Mary Ann Jarrett, 23 Dec. 1850, by J. E. Glenn. Page 59.

William Sapp and Margaret Reid, 19 Feb. 1852, by Jas. Harrod, M.G. Page 59.

J. K. Cunningham and Martha Lasseter, 25 Mar. 1852, by Jas. Harrod, M.G. Page 59.

Curney Turnage and Ann Smith, 28 Mar. 1852, by R. Witherington, J.P. Page 59.

William Hardin and Martha E. Winslett, 8 Jan. 1852, by J. J. Dickson, M.G. Page 59.

James D. Johnson and Ann M. Morrill, 8 Jan. 1852, by J. J. Dickson, M.G. Page 60.

Andrew Saunders and Nancy J. Winslett, 13 Apr. 1852, by A. T. Spence, J.P. Page 60.

Cader A. Parker ordained at Richland Church, Stewart Co., Ga., 3 May 1834. Recorded Barbour Co., 24 Apr. 1852. John Rushing, M.G. & Jas. Lunsford, M.G. Page 60.

William A. McAndrews and Elafar Blakey, 13 Apr. 1852, by Joel
Sims, M.G.   Page 61.

Richard Hill and Eliza M. E. Stephens, 22 Apr. 1852, by M.
Gilchrist, J.P.   Page 61.

John Jordan and Elizar Simkins, 16 Feb. 1851, by W. McCormick,
J.P.   Page 61.

William H. Williams and Margaret A. Jackson, 29 Apr. 1852, by
Jno. Gill Shorter, Judge.   Page 61.

Lewis H. Holmes and Mahala M. Richards, 28 Apr. 1852, by Jesse
W. Corbitt, S.D.   Page 61.

Nathan Reeder and Elizabeth Ann Adkinson, 30 Oct. 1851, by
Aaron Helms.   Page 62.

Peyton Bludworth and Elizabeth A. Ledbetter, 11 Mar. 1852, by
W. McCormick, J.P.   Page 62.

John S. Hamilton and Elizabeth McLean, 24 May 1852, by Asa
Sinquefield, J.P.   Page 62.

William Pearson and Sarah Dukes, 24 May 1852, by M. B. Wellborn,
J.P.   Page 62.

Lewis Edge and Matilda Thomas, 15 Jan. 1852, by E. M. Wilks,
J.P.   Page 62.

Jefferson D. Bludworth and Emily Heron, 13 May 1852, by F. E.
Baker, J.P.   Page 63.

William W. B. Weston ordained at Clayton Baptist Missionary
Church on 1 May 1852.   Presbytery: Andrew Cumbie,
Zacheous Nix, R. R. Rushing and J. S. Dennard.
Page 63.

Erasumas Braley and Rebecca Weaver, 13 May 1852, by Rev. J. J.
Dickson.   Page 63.

John Childra and Lucinda R. Swain, 20 May 1852, by Franklin E.
Baker, J.P.   Page 63.

Squire A. Ham and Elizabeth McLendon, 20 May 1852, by L. L.
Pierce, J.P.   Page 64.

O. P. Slaughter and Eliza Davis, 13 June 1852, by A. T. Spence,
J.P.   Page 64.

Charles J. Jackson and Patience Crowley, 26 June 1852, by D. A.
Norton, J.P.   Page 64.

Thomas Clayton and Dilla Gunnels, 27 June 1852, by Wm. Gallaway,
M.G.   Page 64.

David Ham and Margaret Gann, 12 July 1852, by B. Williams, J.P.
Page 64.

James E. Carr and Elizabeth Bennett, 8 July 1852, by A. T.
Spence, J.P.   Page 65.

Archibald McDonald and Catharine F. S. Glenn, 22 July 1852, by

R. Witherington, J.P.   Page 65.

Charles Pratt and Mary J. Williams, 22 June 1852, by Wm. J.
        Ellis, M.G.   Page 65.

W. H. Heidt and Virginia C. Grisham, 17 June 1852, by Wm. J.
        Ellis, Rector St. James, Eufaula.   Page 65.

William L. Wilkinson and Martha Turnage, 18 June 1852, by M.
        Gilchrist, J.P.   Page 65.

Manning Drew and Elizabeth L. Long, 25 July 1852, by Franklin
        E. Baker, J.P.   Consent of her mother, Melinda
        Long.   Page 66.

Lewis M. Cooper and Nancy Ellis, 28 Feb. 1850, by James Harrod,
        M.G.   Page 66.

Crayton Dicken and Sarah A. E. Calloway, 22 July 1852, by J. J.
        Dickson, M.G.   Page 67.

O. C. Doster and Mary Campbell, 8 Aug. 1852, by Henry Faulk, Jr.,
        J.P.   Page 67.

George W. Carroll and Rhody Thompson, 15 Aug. 1852, by Henry
        Faulk, Jr., J.P.   Page 67.

Charles Winston and Matilda E. Cox, 15 Aug. 1852, by Henry Faulk,
        Jr., J.P.   Page 67.

Theophulius Floyd and Elizabeth Bonds, 26 Aug. 1852, by B.
        Williams, J.P.   Page 67.

Reuben Tucker and Sarah Johnson, 4 Aug. 1852, by D. A. Norton,
        J.P.   Page 67.

Daniel B. Snead and Caroline E. Norton, 31 Aug. 1852, by H. M.
        Tompkins, J.P.   Page 68.

Jeremiah O'Brien and Mrs. Hanna S. J. Sporman, 3 Aug. 1852, by
        Wm. J. Ellis, M.G.   Page 68.

Jesse Kilpatrick and Harriet L. Floyd, 16 Sept. 1852, by Jas.
        Harrod, M.G.   Page 68.

Henry Bowden and Nancy A. Bowden, 23 Sept. 1852, by B. Williams,
        J.P.   Page 68.

George L. Martin and Elizabeth Martin, 24 Sept. 1852, by H. F.
        Reaves, J.P.   Consent of her guardian, John F.
        Martin, for them to intermarry.   Page 69.

Joel DuBose and Angelena Hancock, 13 Sept. 1852, by G. W.
        Williams, J.P.   Page 69.

Ellit Thomas and Ruth C. Bush, 16 Sept. 1852, by G. W. Williams,
        J.P.   Page 69.

George D. Hodge and Ann H. Davis, 26 Sept. 1852, by J. S.
        Dennard, M.G.   Page 69.

James Ross and Katharine McDonald, 22 Sept. 1852, by Henry
        Faulk, J.P.   Page 70.

James Danford and Mary Scott, 7 Oct. 1852, by P. Bludworth, J.P.
Page 70.

Adam Scaines and Susan McLean, 5 Aug. 1852, by L. L. Pierce,
J.P. Page 70.

William Powell and Sarah A. Farmer, 7 Oct. 1852, by J. S. Cole,
J.P. Page 70.

William Long and Emaline Segars, 18 July 1852, by Jesse Holland,
J.P. Page 70.

Jonathan Pope and Mary E. Sanford, 10 Oct. 1852, by G. W.
Williams, J.P. Page 71.

Zachariah Thomas and Drucilla DuBose, 30 Sept. 1852, by G. W.
Williams, J.P. Page 71.

William Later and Ann Ammons, 23 Sept. 1852, by H. Pipkin, J.P.
Page 71.

Johnson Lawless and Charity J. Harvey, 9 Sept. 1852, by M.
Gilchrist, J.P. Page 71.

Sylvester Martin and Susan Williamson, 2 Sept. 1852, by M.
Gilchrist, J.P. Page 71.

John Templer and Charity Hall, 14 Oct. 1852, by H. F. Reaves,
J.P. Consent of her father, Hiram Hall. Page 72.

Henry Z. Telleres and Elizabeth Hinshaw, 10 Oct. 1852, by Henry
Faulk, Jr. Page 72.

Andrew S. Williamson and Elizabeth Wise, 19 Oct. 1852, by Jas.
Gary, J.P. Page 72.

Hiram Helms and Charity Thomas, 16 Sept. 1852, by Uriah W.
Pelham, M.G. Page 72.

Daniel W. Teal and Mary McLeod, 17 Oct. 1852, by M. A.
Patterson, M.G. Page 73.

Thomas W. Howell and Mamie M. Tie, 20 Oct. 1852, by Wm. H.
McIntosh. Page 73.

James R. Hill and Eliza W. Thomas, 17 Oct. 1852, by W. B.
Wellborn, J.P. Page 73.

James Stewart and Charity Padgett, 31 Oct. 1852, by A. T.
Spence, J.P. Consent of his mother, Eliza
Stewart. Page 73.

Duncan McCall and Joanna Warren, 27 Oct. 1852, by Joel Sims,
M.G. Page 73.

John F. Dickinson and Martha Juliet Morton, 18 Nov. 1852, by
G. Malone, M.G. Page 74.

Cornelius Browning and Emily Eidson, 10 Nov. 1852, by L. L.
Pierce, J.P. Page 74.

John N. Danford and Elizabeth McNair, 26 Nov. 1852, by J. S.
Cole, J.P. Page 74.

James Sims and Caroline Johnson, 28 Nov. 1852, by J. S. Cole.
Page 74.

Malcolm Hair and Janeta Bedsole, 28 Oct. 1852, by Wm. H. McIntosh,
M.G. Page 75.

Hughey Gillis and Rhody Ann Duke, 4 Nov. 1852, by G. W.
Williams, J.P. Page 75.

Miller Holliday and Ann Eliza Bell, 28 Nov. 1852, by M. B.
Wellborn, J.P. Page 75.

Edmund Ryal and Mary Hays, 28 Nov. 1852, by A. T. Spence, J.P.
Page 75.

William B. Adams ordained in the M. E. Church at Mobile on 11
Jan. 1852. Recorded 20 Dec. 1852. Page 76.

Robert W. Turner ordained at Bethel Church 14 Sept. 1851.
Recorded 6 Jan. 1853. Presbytery: Isham Hicks,
John Kelly & Thos. T. B. Vicks. Page 76.

Robert H. Anderson and Elizabeth Bennett, 7 Mar. 1852, by
Wesley Vinson, J.P. Page 77.

Henry A. Wyse and Margarett Bryan, 31 Dec. 1851, by Wesley
Vinson, J.P. Page 77.

William H. Stricklin and Elizabeth Jane Thomas, 19 Aug. 1852,
by Wesley Vinson, J.P. Page 77.

Joseph Ellis and Mrs. Mary Wilcox, 9 Sept. 1852, by Wesley
Vinson, J.P. Page 77.

Thomas A. J. Hawkins and Susan B. Hardy, 16 Dec. 1852, by W. B.
Wellborn, J.P. Page 77.

John B. Gilbert and Mrs. Evelina Bright, 13 Jan. 1852, by R. E.
Brown. Page 78.

Samuel Whitsett and Catherine McNeel, 22 Nov. 1852, executed.
Page 78.

William J. Evans and Martha Ivinson, 12 Aug. 1852, by Chas.
Evans, M.G. Page 78.

Franklin B. Lunsford and Harriet E. James, 9 Dec. 1852, by
Edwin James, M.G. Page 78.

Chappell Hall and Mary C. Walker, 4 Nov. 1852, by H. F. Reaves,
J.P. Page 78.

William Odom and Elizabeth Hall, 17 Nov. 1852, by H. F. Reaves,
J.P. Page 78.

Jesse R. Braswell and Mary Taylor, 3 Dec. 1852, by H. F. Reaves,
J.P. Page 79.

Patrick Hallin and Almedam Bartlett, 15 Dec. 1852, by M. B.
Wellborn, J.P. Page 79.

J. C. Varadore and Susan A. Bryan, 26 Nov. 1852, by D. A.
Norton, J.P. Page 79.

William P. Sanders and Margarett C. Farmer, 9 Jan. 1853, by L. L.
        Pierce, J.P. Page 79.

William L. Wise and Frances J. Purswell, 6 Jan. 1853, by L. L.
        Pierce, J.P. Page 79.

Lewis B. Norton and Rosanna Cox, 23 Dec. 1852, by B. Williams,
        J.P. Page 79.

Felix Holder and Catherine Spurger, 9 Dec. 1852, by F. E. Baker,
        J.P. Page 80.

William M. Aikens and Caroline Parker, 19 Dec. 1852, by Franklin
        E. Baker, J.P. Page 80.

John M. Hill and Sarah A. Laseter, 2 Dec. 1852, by D. A. Norton,
        J.P. Page 80.

William T. Lunsford and Sarah E. James, 18 Nov. 1852, by Edwin
        James, M.G. Page 80.

James B. James and Susan G. Lunsford, 5 Jan. 1853, by Edwin
        James, M.G. Page 80.

John Parson and Sarah Reynolds, 31 Dec. 1852, by Edwin James,
        M.G. Page 81.

James R. Towler and Sarah Williams, 27 Dec. 1852, by Asa
        Sinquefield, J.P. Page 81.

Joseph Powell and Matilda Thorn, 2 Jan. 1853, by Henry Faulk,
        Jr., J.P. Page 81.

John Daniels and Rebeca Tharp, 12 Dec. 1852, by Henry Faulk, Jr.,
        J.P. Page 81.

W. A. Bryan and Susan Sinquefield, 27 Dec. 1852, by W. R. Cowen,
        Judge. Page 81.

William J. Ranton and Kisiah Cureton, 26 Aug. 1852, by Wesley
        Vinson, J.P. Page 82.

John C. Craigg and Nancy Cureton, 30 Sept. 1852, by Wesley
        Vinson, J.P. Page 82.

Burton L. Dickens and Mary E. Vinson, 12 May 1852, by Charles
        Evans, J.P. Page 82.

Milton D. Barnes and Polly Hollimon, 24 Aug. 1852, by Wesley
        Vinson, J.P. Page 82.

John W. Purvis and Martha Young, 20 Jan. 1853, by Gabrul
        Purswell, J.P.   Consent of his father, David B.
        Purvis. Page 82.

Robert A. Price and Miss Z. A. Helms, issued 18 Jan. 1853,
        return not recorded. Page 83.

John J. Price and Sarah A. Grubbs, 20 Jan. 1853, by R. E. Brown,
        M.G.   Consent of her father, William Grubbs.
        Page 83.

Thomas J. Price and Miss M. H. Jennings, 20 Jan. 1853, by

H. Pipkin, J.P. Page 83.

A. H. Sanders and Nancy Stevenson, 13 Jan. 1853, by B. D.
            Loveless, M.G. Page 84.

James F. Childree and Mary Greathouse, issued 22 Jan. 1853,
            return not recorded. Consent of her father,
            Allerson M. Greathouse. Page 84.

Tilverton J. Bradly and Nancy A. Carrington, 26 Jan. 1853, by
            M. Gilchrist, J.P. Page 85.

Calvin Seay and Sophrona Cody, 27 Jan. 1853, by Oliver Fleming,
            M.G. Page 85.

F. M. Odom and Elizabeth Nicholdson, 1 Feb. 1853, by B.
            Williams, J.P. Page 85.

David L. White and Clesly V. H. Brown, 16 Dec. 1852, by R. E.
            Brown, M.G. Page 86.

William M. Holt and Lucy A. Fortson, 3 Feb. 1853, by J. J.
            Harris. Consent of her father, T. W. Fortson.
            Page 86.

George Taylor and Margarett Glass, 3 Feb. 1853, by Jas. Harrod,
            M.G. Consent of his mother, Mary Cameron. Page
            86.

Jesse J. Harrold and Frances Langford, 9 Jan. 1853, by M. B.
            Wellborn, J.P. Page 87.

Owen Haley and Susan Dickson, 6 Feb. 1853, by W. R. Cowan,
            Judge. Page 87.

William H. McIntosh ordained in the Baptist faith on the 3rd
            Lord's Day in 1836, at South Newport, in McIntosh
            County, Georgia. Recorded 12 Feb. 1853.
            Presbytery: Samuel L. Law, Jas. McDonald & Josiah
            S. Law. Page 87.

George W. Simpkins and Susan Hicks, 14 Feb. 1853, by Thos. T. B.
            Vickers. Consent of parents, Samuel Simpkins and
            William B. Hicks. Page 88.

John D. Collins ordained at Antioch Baptist Church in Jones
            County, Georgia, on 5 Nov. 1842. Recorded 17 Feb.
            1853. Luke Newell, Mod. & Jas. P. Lowe, Clk.
            Page 88.

William Flowers and Rebeca Reaves, 13 Feb. 1853, by H. F.
            Reaves, J.P. Page 88.

Robert W. Barr and Harriet A. Farrar, 21 Feb. 1853, by P. C.
            Winn. Page 89.

H. B. Ryan and Malinda A. Mann, 22 Dec. 1852, by M. A. Patterson,
            M.G. Page 89.

Franklin Singleton and Martha McCall, 24 Feb. 1853, by J. S.
            Cole, J.P. Consent of his mother, Polly
            Williamson, and her father, Daniel McCall. Page
            89.

W. M. Bates and Martha Morrison, 1 Mar. 1853, by Mark S. Andrews, M.G. Page 90.

Aaron M. Hinson and Nancy Price, 27 Feb. 1853, by B. Williams, J.P. Page 90.

B. W. W. Bell and Temperance Brazzil, 3 Mar. 1853, by W. R. Owen, Judge of Probate. Page 90.

W. S. Houston and Louiza D. Bradly, 10 Mar. 1853, by H. F. Reaves, J.P. Page 91.

Abner G. Childree and Elizabeth Greathouse, 10 Jan. 1853, by Franklin E. Baker, J.P. Page 91.

Allen Daniels and Catherine Minshew, 6 Mar. 1853, by Henry Faulk, Jr., J.P. Page 91.

John Barber and Eveline Mathews, 1 Feb. 1853, by Henry Faulk, Jr., J.P. Page 92.

David D. Graves and Bethany Avery, 16 Jan. 1853, by Henry Faulk, Jr., J.P. Page 92.

William Shipp and Nancy Feagin, 17 Mar. 1853, by J. J. Dickson, M.G. Page 93.

Giles C. Efurd and Martha Collins, 19 Dec. 1852, by P. Bludworth, J.P. Page 93.

George W. Moore and Eliza J. Giddings, 31 Mar. 1853, by Thos. F. Bludworth, J.P. Page 93.

Goldwire G. Hill and Geneavin S. Jones, 3 Apr. 1853, by Z. J. Daniel, J.P. Page 94.

N. L. Hudson and Nancy A. Harris, 3 Apr. 1853, by Thos. P. Crymes. Page 94.

A. L. Gaston and Mary C. Sinquefield, 5 Apr. 1853, by Wm. H. McIntosh, M.G. Page 94.

George W. Holland and Nancy E. Webber, 7 Apr. 1853, at Richard Webber's, by Edwin James, M.G. Page 95.

Patrick McDonald and Sarah A. Heulette, 17 Mar. 1853, by Henry Faulk, Jr., J.P. Page 95.

John W. King and Sarah Shiner, 31 Mar. 1853, by Henry Faulk, Jr., J.P. Page 95.

Phillip Childs and Alsey Pettis, 7 Apr. 1853, by Henry Faulk, Jr., J.P. Page 96.

Thomas H. Moody and Margarett Ann Highsmith, 14 Apr. 1853, by H. Pipkin, J.P. Page 96.

Edmond Womble and Rebeca Adkins, 7 Apr. 1853, by D. M. Weston, J.P. Page 96.

A. M. Faison and Elizabeth F. Owen, 9 Apr. 1853, at Dr. W. J. Owen's, by W. A. McCarta. Page 97.

W. A. Bennett and Miss C. A. Mallory, 17 Feb. 1853, by J. J. Dickson, M.G. Page 97.

Daniel D. James and Nancy A. Wilson, 28 Apr. 1853, by Edwin James, M.G. Page 97.

Hilery Hooks and Charlott C. Merit, 16 Dec. 1852, by J. J. Dickson, M.G. Page 97.

George G. B. Faulk and Martha Sheppard, 4 Aug. 1852, by Jesse Holland, J.P. Page 98.

John McLane and Lila Wood, 13 Mar. 1853, by W. N. Adkinson, J.P. Page 98.

Westly McKenzie and Sarah Smith, 25 Apr. 1852, by W. N. Adkinson, J.P. Page 98.

Pleasant L. Albritian and Rebeca China, 9 May 1853, by B. A. Brown, J.P. Consent of his father, Lanier Albritian. Page 98.

James B. Hearin and Rachael Raburg, 15 Nov. 1852, by E. W. Wilks, J.P. Page 99.

William Faison and Laura Whittington, 13 May 1853, by Jas. Gary, J.P. Page 99.

Joseph Wells and Sarah Gunterson, 23 May 1853, by Jack Hardman, J.P. Consent of her mother, Martha Gunterson. Page 99.

George F. Allen and Elizabeth M. Wells, 25 May 1853, by A. E. Jones. Consent of her parents, Willis and Mary Huddleston. Page 100.

Major L. Sayers and Sarah A. Robinson, 26 May 1853, by Ira Britt, J.P. Page 100.

William Morrison and Margarett Hagler, 28 May 1853, by Jas. S. Baxter, J.P. Page 100.

George W. Thompson and Josephine Austin, 14 June 1853, by Thompson S. Glenn. Consent of her father, A. B. Austin. Page 101.

Thomas H. Ellis and Mary E. Thornton, 16 Dec. 1852, by James Griffith, M.G. Page 101.

Samuel Vining and Mary A. McBride, 17 June 1853, by J. J. Dickson. Page 101.

William A. J. Langston and Elizabeth Screws, 26 June 1853, by G. Malone. Consent of her father, Jacob Screws, for her to intermarry. Page 101.

Edward Justice and Ann Bird, 30 June 1853, by J. J. Dickson, M.G. Page 102.

William S. Smith and Caroline A. Hall, 26 June 1853, by Silas A. Stokes, J.P. Consent of her mother, Florina Hall. Page 102.

Allen Jacobs and Easter Ann Carter, 29 June 1853, by Henry
          Faulk, Jr., J.P. Consent of her father, John
          Carter. Page 103.

Adison D. Cleckley and Mary H. F. Scott, 5 July 1853, by Wm. A.
          McCarty. Page 103.

Henry C. Snipes and Margarett R. Cunningham, 14 July 1853, at D.
          Cunningham's, by M. A. Patterson. Consent of his
          mother, Mariah A. Snipes. Pages 103 & 104.

Thomas Berry and Caroline V. Truetlin, 14 Oct. 1852, by John C.
          Carter. Page 104.

William S. Rackley and Ann E. Blount, 12 Oct. 1852, by A. S.
          Glenn. Page 104.

John Littlefield and Jane Grubbs, 13 July 1853, by R. N. Lowe,
          J.P. Consent of his father, Henry E. Littlefield,
          and her mother, Margaret Grubbs. Page 104.

W. G. Lomar and Mary E. DuBose, 14 July 1853, by Thos. P.
          Crymes. Page 105.

John F. Ingram and Louisa Blalock, 21 July 1853, by Jas. Gary,
          J.P. Page 105.

Ezekeal Alexander and Mrs. Sarah Tucker, 21 July 1853, by G. W.
          Purnell, M.G. Page 105.

J. W. Thorn and Martha Davis, 28 July 1853, by Henry Faulk, Jr.,
          J.P. Page 106.

Harvey Lee and Nancy Wise, 1 Aug. 1853, at Epham Wise's, by
          Silas A. Stokes, J.P. Page 106.

M. M. N. McEathern and Nancy Green, 4 Aug. 1853, by M. A.
          Patterson, M.G. Page 106.

William Palmer and Ann Cheesbro, 5 Aug. 1853, by Wm. B. Neal,
          Elder of M. E. Church. Page 107.

Epamendas Woods and Sarah Caroline McBride, 18 Aug. 1853, by
          Z. J. Daniel, J.P. Consent of her mother, Mary
          Vining. Page 107.

Mathew Owens and Elvira L. Anglin, 11 Aug. 1853, by W. R. Cowen,
          Judge. Consent of her father, William Anglin.
          Page 107.

John McNaughton and Cornilia J. Streeter, 18 Aug. 1853, by M.
          Gilchrist, J.P. Page 108.

F. J. Adams and Sarah Jane Seay, 25 Aug. 1853, by Thos. F.
          Bludworth, J.P. Page 108.

Turner Johnson and Margarett Earp, 1 Sept. 1853, at Flewellen
          Earp's, by F. E. Baker, J.P. Page 108.

Stephen G. Whatley and Sarah Ann Hammock, issued 3 Sept. 1853,
          return not recorded. Page 109.

John Connell and Sarah Beasley, 6 Sept. 1853, by P. Bludworth,

J.P.   Page 109.

Michael Lightner and Martha Hollis, 6 Sept. 1853, at M.
        Lightner's, by Judge W. R. Cowen.   Page 109.

Nathaniel Snell and Mary C. Condry, 8 Sept. 1853, by L. L.
        Pierce, J.P.   Page 110.

Hardy B. McClendon and Laura Danforth, 8 Sept. 1853, by Wm. B.
        Neal.   Consent of her guardian. Charles Petty.
        Page 110.

P. F. Posey and Amanda Silas, issued 9 Sept. 1853, return not
        recorded.   Page 110.

Harvey Anglin and Laura Ann Seay, 13 Sept. 1853, by F. E. Baker.
        Consent of his father, Wm. Anglin, and her parents,
        H. M. & Ann Seay.   Page 111.

F. A. McAplin and Epsey Williamson, 15 Sept. 1853, by M.
        Gilchrist, J.P.   Page 111.

Alexander Robinson and Julia Ann Mitchell, 15 Sept. 1853, by
        D. M. Weston, J.P.   Page 111.

Alexander Atwell and Elizabeth Williams, issued 13 Sept. 1853,
        return not recorded.   Page 112.

Samuel M. Covington and Mary A. Tye, 18 Sept. 1853, by Joel
        Sims, M.G.   Page 112.

John H. Perkins and Mary A. B. Craig, 22 Sept. 1853, at Lovick
        Craig's, by Thos. P. Crymes.   Page 112.

James S. Rogers and Elizabeth A. Bryan, 22 Sept. 1853, by W. R.
        Cowen, Judge of Probate.   Page 113.

James R. Barnett and Juliet A. Daniel, 4 Oct. 1853, at Glenn-
        ville, by P. C. Hearn, M.G.   Page 113.

Archabald C. Wise and Mrs. Elvira D. Martin, 6 Oct. 1853, by
        Wm. H. McIntosh, M.G.   Page 113.

William Sims and Marthy Searcy, 13 Oct. 1853, by Z. Wood, J.P.
        Page 114.

Alexander McNair and Sarah W. Miller, 12 Oct. 1853, by A.
        McMillan, M.G.   Consent of her grandmother,
        Nancy Herrington.   Page 114.

Edmond Danford and Nancy Scroggins, 13 Oct. 1853, at Jas.
        Scroggins', by R. N. Lowe, J.P.   Page 115.

F. W. Bryan and Sarah E. Rogers, 13 Oct. 1853, by Edwin James,
        M.G.   Consent of her father, Cornilius Rogers.
        Page 115.

Jacob Williams and Peny DuBose, 21 Oct. 1853, by R. N. Lowe,
        J.P.   Page 115.

William Wynn and Catherine Martin, 16 Oct. 1853, by R. N. Lowe,
        J.P.   Page 116.

Samuel C. Bradley ordained at Ramah Baptist Church in Barbour
        County on 26 Feb. 1853. James Griffith & Wm.
        W. B. Weston. Page 116.

Irby L. Holt and Josephine Ivy, 25 Oct. 1853, by John Crowell,
        M.G. Page 116.

Alexander W. Stinson and Louisetin A. Talbot, 23 Oct. 1853, by
        G. W. Purnell, M.G. Page 116.

William Hall and Mrs. Martha Campbell, 26 Oct. 1853, by Miles
        McInnis, J.P. Page 117.

Henry H. Field, Jr. and Sarah C. McRae, 3 Nov. 1853, by M. A.
        Patterson, M.G. Page 117.

Micjah Marcus and Jane Smothers, 3 Nov. 1853, at Crouker
        Smothers', by Z. Wood, J.P. Page 117.

Cornelius Williams and Martha J. Holly, 3 Nov. 1853, by Solomon
        Sikes, M.G. Page 118.

Rubin Sanders and Sarah V. Reaves, 13 Nov. 1853, by James Gary,
        J.P. Page 118.

William C. Wallace and Leonora F. Booth, 17 Nov. 1853, by Mark
        S. Andrews, M.G. Consent of her mother, Martha
        R. W. Booth. Page 118.

William M. Avant and Mary Ann Day, 17 Nov. 1853, at Ranson
        Day's, by Lovard L. Pierce, J.P. Page 119.

Dr. B. F. Oens and Rebecca Rivers, 17 Nov. 1853, by P. C. Wynn,
        M.G. Consent of her father, Thomas Rivers. Page
        119.

Robert F. Wilkins and Mrs. Caroline Sheppard, 17 Nov. 1853, by
        D. A. Norton, J.P. Page 120.

Bryant B. Bailey and Rebecca Flowers, 17 Nov. 1853, by D. A.
        Bush. Consent of his mother, Hosea Bailey. Page
        120.

A. H. H. Phillips and Martha B. Porter, 24 Nov. 1853, at Richard
        Porter's, by Henry Faulk, J.P. Page 120.

Charles S. Williamson and Adeline Evans, 10 Oct. 1853, at Wm.
        Evans', by A. E. Jones, J.P. Page 121.

Nathan L. Robinson and Emily F. Fleming, 22 Nov. 1853, at J.
        Fleming's, by L. L. Pierce, J.P. Page 121.

Andrew J. White and Sarah E. McLauchlin, 24 Nov. 1853, by Z. J.
        Daniel, J.P. Consent of her father, A. McLauch-
        lin. Page 121.

Thomas H. Roberts and Ann White, 1 Dec. 1853, by P. C. Winn, M.G.
        Page 122.

Young Smith and Frances Crow, 3 June 1853, by Z. Wood, J.P.
        Page 122.

John C. Beasley and Mary Taylor, 8 Dec. 1853, at Joshua Taylor's, by B. Williams, J.P.   Page 122.

Jesse M. Shepard and Asamariah R. Parker, 8 Dec. 1853, at Joel
     P. Parker's, by F. E. Baker, J.P.   Page 122.

Hatch Cook and Elizabeth Brown, 15 Dec. 1853, by William J.
     Ellis.   Page 123.

Mathew A. Leveret and Miss L. R. Cowart, 14 Dec. 1853, by Oliver
     Fleming, M.G.   Consent of her father, John E.
     Cowart.   Page 123.

Robert Andrews and Sarah King, 11 Dec. 1853, at W. King's, by
     R. E. Brown, M.G.   Page 123.

Elisha Hall and Delilah Sheppard, 11 Dec. 1853, by D. A. Norton,
     J.P.   Consent of her father, John Sheppard.   Page
     123.

T. J. Green and Mahaley J. Hill, 22 Dec. 1853, executed.   Page
     124.

Angus McA. Williams and Menerva E. Alexander, 15 Dec. 1853, at
     Ezekeal Alexander's, by Edward Cody, M.G.   Page
     124.

James R. Clark and Darcus Crocker, 13 Dec. 1853, by W. R. Cowen,
     Judge of Probate.   Page 125.

Alexander D. McRae and Elizabeth McRae, 15 Dec. 1853, at J. R.
     McRae's, by P. Bludworth, J.P.   Page 125.

John B. Warr and Elizabeth Jane Price, 18 Dec. 1853, by L. L.
     Pierce, J.P.   Consent of her father, Bunel Price.
     Page 125.

Thomas Crew and Elizabeth Guice, 21 Dec. 1853, by C. A. Parker,
     M.G.   Page 126.

Thomas McElvan and Margarett Hall, 28 Dec. 1853, by T. S. Glenn.
     Page 126.

James Miller and Mary Kent, 21 Dec. 1853, at Avery Kent's, by
     A. E. Jones, J.P.   Page 126.

Ranson Powell and Margarett Stephens, 22 Dec. 1853, at David
     Powell's, by Miles McInnis, J.P.   Page 127.

Albert Rees and Mary A. R. Griffin, 22 Dec. 1853, at Mr.
     Griffin's, by M. R. Sims, J.P.   Page 127.

Joseph F. Robson and Elizabeth Marlor, 25 Dec. 1853, by C. A.
     Parker, M.G.   Page 127.

Andrew J. Murray and Margarett A. Jones, 22 Dec. 1853, by G. W.
     Purnell, M.G.   Consent of her father, James
     Jones.   Page 128.

James C. Warren and Susanah Hendley, 22 Dec. 1853, at Wm.
     Hendley's, by B. A. Barron, J.P.   Page 128.

W. S. Johnson and Elizabeth Register, 25 Dec. 1853, by F. E.
     Baker, J.P.   Consent of her mother and step-father,

Jeptha and Ludy Ann Lindsey. Page 128.

John S. Delashaw and Mary Campbell, 24 Dec. 1853, by L. L.
        Pierce, J.P. Page 129.

Joseph Sumersett and Lucinda Jones, 22 Dec. 1853, at Mr. Jones',
        by W. R. Cowen, Judge. Page 129.

James W. Cawthorn and Nancy J. Blair, 29 Dec. 1853, at William
        Blair's, by Jas. Harrod, M.G.   Consent of his
        guardian, Ritchard Knight. Page 130.

W. A. B. Lawson and Mrs. Sarah A. Thomas, 27 Dec. 1853, at
        Jacob Lampley's, by Wm. McCormick, J.P. Page 130.

Aaron Helms and Mary Whigham, 3 Jan. 1854, at Joseph Whigham's,
        by Jno. D. Collins. Page 130.

Benjamin Wright and Nancy McSwean, 28 Dec. 1853, by W. N.
        Adkinson, J.P. Page 131.

George P. Pittman and Mary A. E. Walden, 1 Jan. 1854, by Z.
        Wood, J.P.   Consent of her father, Albert Walden.
        Page 131.

Henry C. Ward and Miss L. A. Warren, 1 Jan. 1854, by Wm. B. Neal.
        Consent of her mother, Nancy Loveless. Page 132.

William McGuire and Ann E. Rivers, 1 Jan. 1854, by B. H. Banks.
        Page 132.

James W. Cameron and Matilda Nolin, 3 Jan. 1854, by A. E. Jones,
        J.P. Page 132.

William M. Hardwick and Louisa J. Richards, 5 Jan. 1854, by Z.
        Wood. Page 133.

James Parmer and Mary B. Bullock, 5 Jan. 1854, at John Bullock's,
        by A. E. Jones, J.P. Page 133.

William E. Smith and Amanda Epperson, 5 Jan. 1854, at Young
        Smith's, by T. S. Glenn. Page 133.

Will D. Hill and Sarah E. Marshall, 5 Jan. 1854, at T. Marshall's,
        by T. S. Glenn. Page 134.

George Bradham and Sarah Emerson, 5 Jan. 1854, at B. H.
        Emerson's, by Elder Wm. Lee. Page 134.

John M. Johnson and Sarah A. Wilkinson, 13 Jan. 1854, at S.
        Wilkinson's, by A. Helms. Page 134.

Michael Cody and Francis C. R. Thornton, 10 Jan. 1854, by H.
        Pipkin, J.P.   Consent of her father, J. M.
        Thornton. Page 135.

Adam Hagler and Martha J. Bishop, 19 Jan. 1854, at Isam Deas',
        by Miles McInnis, J.P. Page 135.

Abram Brumbelow and Sarah Hagler, 12 Jan. 1854, at Jacob
        Hagler's, by Miles McInnis, J.P. Page 135.

Solomon Hargroves and Tobitha J. Tucker, 12 Jan. 1854, at Jas.

Tucker's, by Jno. L. Williams, J.P. Page 136.

Richard Morris and Jane C. Lewis, issued 21 Jan. 1854, return
not recorded. Page 136.

S. C. Marly and Miss S. M. Pierce, 8 Feb. 1854, at L. L.
Pierce's, by D. McGilvary, J.P. Page 137.

Tandy W. King and Louisa Efurd, 24 Jan. 1854, at T. C. Efurd's,
by F. E. Baker, J.P. Page 137.

Dosier Cade and Mary F. Cade, 24 Jan. 1854, by A. C. Parker, M.G.
Page 137.

James Seagars and Martha A. McCaller, 25 Jan. 1854, at Neal
McCaller's, by Miles McInnis, J.P. Page 138.

Daniel Warren and Amanda J. Dukes, 2 Feb. 1854, at David Dukes',
by W. R. Cowen, Judge. Page 138.

Nathaniel Walker and Martha Smith, issued 30 Jan. 1854, return
not recorded. Page 138.

John Cunningham and Christian Gillis, 2 Feb. 1854, by Jno. L.
Williams, J.P. Page 139.

James Adams and Mary J. Wood, 5 Feb. 1854, by J. M. White, J.P.
Page 139.

Charles Buckhats and Susan Myrick, 1 Feb. 1854, by B. Williams,
J.P. Page 139.

Malcom McLean and Martha Smith, issued 2 Feb. 1854, return not
recorded. Page 139.

James A. Arnold and Cynthia Bass, 19 Feb. 1854, by W. A.
McCarty. Page 140.

James L. Lowman and Martha E. Lowman, 9 Feb. 1854, at Mrs.
Lowman's, by Thos. P. Crymes. Page 140.

Fredrick C. McDaniel and Esther R. Flinn, 5 Feb. 1854, at John
Flinn's, by W. McCormick, J.P. Page 140.

W. H. B. Mosher and Mariah A. Hill, 16 Feb. 1854, by Z. J.
Daniel, J.P. Consent of her father, Martin M.
Hill. Page 141.

N. A. Petty and Nancy Ann Norton, 13 Feb. 1854, by Judge W. R.
Cowen. Consent of her mother, Isabella Norton.
Page 141.

Lewis J. Hunt and Susan E. M. Bradbery, 16 Feb. 1854, at G. W.
Hunt's, by Z. J. Daniel, J.P. Page 142.

W. Lambert and Elizabeth Dukes, 16 Feb. 1854, at William Dukes',
by Z. Wood, J.P. Page 142.

Andrew H. Beauchamp and Margarett E. Allen, 21 Feb. 1854, at
Eufaula, by Jas. Story. Consent of her father,
G. S. Allen. (p. 144). Page 142.

Reubin Singleton and Louisa Jones, 19 Feb. 1854, at Eufaula, by

Edwin James, M.G.   Page 143.

John Smith and Anna Jane McNeil, 27 Feb. 1854, by F. E. Baker,
J.P.   Page 143.

James Slack and Rebecca White, 1 Mar. 1854, by Z. J. Daniel,
J.P.   Consent of her father, Willis White.   Page
143.

L. M. Allen and Mary Kilpatrick, 26 Feb. 1854, by Z. J. Daniel,
J.P.   Page 144.

Willis Williams and Margarett McCrary, 26 Feb. 1854, by W. H.
Cowen, Judge.   Page 144.

John Quattlebum and Margaret J. McDaniel, 5 Mar. 1854, by Thos.
F. Bludworth, J.P.   Page 144.

Robert Dill and Elizabeth P. Laney, 15 Mar. 1854, at Eufaula,
by W. J. Ellis, M.G.   Page 145.

Samuel W. Wallace and Maldonta Cowan, 22 Mar. 1854, at Eufaula,
by Jas. Story.   Consent of Dr. Cowan.   Page 145.

Thomas Ventress and Mary A. Norton, 21 Mar. 1854, at J. R.
Norton's, by W. R. Cowen, Judge.   Page 145.

James W. Norton and Ruth M. M. A. J. Maxwell, 28 Mar. 1854, by
W. K. Norton, M.G.   Page 146.

Andrew Evans and Elizabeth Howell, 5 Apr. 1854, at Washington
Howell's, by A. E. Jones, J.P.   Page 146.

Uriah Hammock and Artimitia Tye, 13 Apr. 1854, by J. L.
Williams, J.P.   Consent of her parents, John and
Mary Tye.   Page 146.

Robert P. Boulware and Miss W. T. Fraser, 14 Apr. 1854, at Dr.
Boulware's, by C. A. Parker, M.G.   Page 147.

W. M. Davis ordained at Cowikee Baptist Church, Barbour County,
on 16 Apr. 1854.   Recorded 22 Apr. 1854.   Joel
Sims, W. H. McIntosh, James Griffith, & B. D.
Loveless.   Page 147.

William McLeod and Catherine McRae, 23 Apr. 1854, at C. M.
McRae's, by P. Bludworth, J.P.   Page 147.

Worthy G. Grubbs and Sarah Loveless, 27 Apr. 1854, at B. D.
Loveless', by Judge W. H. Cowen.   Page 148.

L. H. Brown and Mary J. Rouse, 30 Apr. 1854, at Clayton, by
Wm. B. Neal, T.E.   Page 148.

H. G. Spear and Miss E. C. Wright, 11 May 1854, at Jno. Wright's,
by Oliver F. Fleming, M.G.   Page 148.

Henry S. Shorter and Adrianna C. Keitt, 9 May 1854, in Eufaula,
by W. H. McIntosh, M.G.   Page 149.

Peter Cunningham and Amanda Williams, 11 May 1854, at Jno. L.
Williams', by D. A. Bush, J.P.   Page 149.

Thomas Coles and Laura M. Shorter, 9 May 1854, by W. H. McIntosh, M.G.   Consent of her mother, Mary B. Shorter. Page 149.

Hartwell Collins and Louisa Williams, 9 May 1854, at Buckner Williams', by Wm. B. Neal, T.E.   Page 150.

Daniel Beasley and Malinda M. Capel, 14 May 1854, at Jas. Capel's, by Wm. McCormick, J.P.   Page 150.

John Edgler and Francis Eubanks, 25 May 1854, at Mary Eubanks', by G. W. Carter, M.G.   Page 150.

John Hardy and Margarett D. Kinchen, 25 May 1854, at Mr. Kinchen's, by G. W. Purnell, M.G.   Page 150.

Solomon Butler and Fanny Anderson, 6 June 1854 by L. L. Pierce, J.P.   Page 151.

James Hinson and Louise M. Rutland, 1 June 1854, at Reddin Rutland's, by Jas. Harrod, M.G.   Page 151.

Henry F. Turner and Mary Jane Cobb, 4 June 1854, by J. M. White, J.P.   Consent of her mother, Harriet W. Cobb. Page 151.

Seaborn Reynolds and Francis Thomas, 4 June 1854, by Edwin James, M.G.   Consent of his step-father, John Persons.   Page 152.

James E. Scroggins and Ann E. Harrell, 6 June 1854, by R. N. Lowe, J.P.   Consent of her mother, Mary Ann G. Harrell.   Page 152.

Edwin W. Allen and Sarah A. D. King, 13 Jan. 1854, by Jas. H. Mallard.   Page 153.

Francis M. Arrington and Sarah E. Stephens, 14 June 1854, at W. Stephen's, by R. N. Lowe, J.P.   Page 153.

J. H. Pearson and Mrs. Martha Brooks, 28 June 1854, at F. E. Baker's, by F. E. Baker.   Page 153.

James F. Durden and Nancy Forehand, 29 June 1854, at Stephen Forehand's, by Edwin James, M.G.   Page 154.

Benjamin F. Petty and Mary E. Lee, 27 June 1854, at N. Lee's, by Wm. B. Neal, T.E.   Page 154.

J. J. Price and Martha Maloy, 6 July 1854, at Duncan Maloy's, by H. Pipkin, J.P.   Page 154.

Laird F. McMurry and Manerva J. Sims, 20 July 1854, by W. R. Cowen, Judge of Probate.   Page 154.

Moses Pridgen and Mrs. Amanda M. Hatcher, issued 21 July 1854, return not recorded.   Page 155.

William Clark and Menerva Palmer, 27 July 1854, at Geo. W. Palmer's, by Z. Wood, J.P.   Consent of his father, John Clark.   Page 155.

John H. Dent and Fanny A. Whipple, 25 July 1854, by Wm. B. Neal,

T.E.   Page 155.

Faknard C. McRae and Mary Ann E. Cameron, 27 July 1854, by Miles
      McInnis, J.P. Page 156.

Turner Howell and Mary Jane Wise, 4 Aug. 1854, at Ezkeal Wise's,
      by A. E. Jones, J.P. Page 156.

Edwin T. Sherman and Louisa M. Conner, 10 Aug. 1854, by Jas. W.
      Shores, M.G. Page 156.

Micajah Smothers and Lucinda Susan Watkins, 17 Aug. 1854, by J.
      Richards, J.P. Consent of their parents, C.
      Smothers and James Watkins. Page 157.

Josiah Winburn and Emily A. M. Warr, 13 Aug. 1854, by L. L.
      Pierce, J.P. Consent of her parents, John and
      Nancy Warr. Page 157.

George W. Dudley and Emeline Alexander, 22 Aug. 1854, at W. E.
      Alexander's, by Jas. Story. Page 157.

Thomas E. Nix and Virginia Peak, 20 Aug. 1854, by Wm. M. Davis,
      M.G. Consent of her guardian, J. D. Johnson.
      Page 158.

Jackson Odum and Mrs. Ann Ryals, 20 Aug. 1854, at Louisville,
      by B. F. Beverly. Page 158.

William R. Cowen and Elizabeth C. Clark, 20 Aug. 1854, at J.
      Clark's, by W. B. Neal, T.E. Page 159.

Emanuel Johnson and Ann Elizabeth Hightower, 5 Sept. 1854, by
      B. Williams. Consent of her father, Thomas A.
      Hightower. Page 159.

Benjamin Parmer, Jr. and Emily Eliza Key, 10 Sept. 1854, by A. E.
      Jones, J.P. Consent of her parents, Thomas and
      Eliza Key. Page 159.

Hugh McGilvary and Effa McLeod, 10 Sept. 1854, at Malcom McLeod's,
      by D. McGilvary, J.P. Page 160.

Nathan Williams and Lany Miller, 12 Sept. 1854, at Saml. Nixon's,
      by T. W. Richards, J.P. Page 160.

Henry Smith and Anna C. McEachern, 21 Sept. 1854, at Gilbert
      McEachern's, by M. A. Patterson. Page 160.

John S. Parker and Cyntha A. Clark, 21 Sept. 1854, by Wright
      Flowers. Page 161.

Austin C. Cargill and Prescilla Preast, 1 Oct. 1854, in Eufaula,
      by J. W. Jordan, M.G. Page 161.

William Ott and Sarah A. Lawhorn, 28 Sept. 1854, at W. Lawhorn's,
      by G. Malone, M.G. Page 161.

William P. Lester and Mary Jane Dansby, 28 Sept. 1854, at Isam
      M. Dansby's, by Miles McInnis, J.P. Page 162.

John A. English and Florence Ricks, 5 Oct. 1854, at Mr. Ricks,
      by G. W. Purnell, M.G. Page 162.

Judge Parrish and Mary Grice, 1 Oct. 1854, by B. Williams, J.P.
Page 162.

J. T. Wright and Sarah J. Stripling, 18 Oct. 1854, at James
Stripling's, by J. Shanks, M.G. Page 163.

Thomas A. Stephens and Loicy McCarroll, 5 Oct. 1854, at Mary
McCarroll's, by L. L. Pierce, J.P. Page 163.

John B. Potts and Sarah Payne, 10 Oct. 1854, at Jos. Payne's,
by A. E. Payne. Consent of parents, John Potts
and Joseph Payne. Page 163.

Nathan H. Lindsey and Martha A. M. Earp, 12 Oct. 1854, by F. E.
Baker, J.P. Consent of his father Jeptha Lindsey.
Page 164.

L. W. Price and Elizabeth J. Horn, 15 Oct. 1854, by L. L.
Pierce, J.P. Consent of their parents, Burrel
Price and Nathan Horn. Page 164.

Malcom Carmichael and Pennelia A. McLeary, 12 Oct. 1854, at Mary
E. McLeary's, by B. Williams, J.P. Page 165.

John LeCount and Caroline Cameron, 19 Oct. 1854, at L. Cameron's,
by H. Pipkin, J.P. Page 165.

William Furman, Jr. and Julia E. DuBose, 9 Nov. 1854, at
Glennville, by W. A. McCarty. Consent of her
father, E. E. DuBose. Page 165.

Daniel M. McLeod and Mary Temple, 19 Oct. 1854, at Mrs. Temple's,
by Jas. Harrod, M.G. Page 166.

Columbus Herring and Catherine Utsey, 19 Oct. 1854, at Jacob
Utsey's, by Wm. McCormick, J.P. Page 166.

James J. Davis and Mary A. Hardman, 26 Oct. 1854, by Francis M.
Grace, M.G. Consent of her father, Jack Hardman.
Page 167.

James D. Faison and Julia A. Owen, 28 Nov. 1854, by W. H.
Ellison, M.G. Consent of her father, J. W. Owen.
Page 167.

Jesse Holland and Harriet Brumbelow, 23 Oct. 1854, at Wm.
Holland's, by Jas. S. Baxter, J.P. Consent of
her parents, Jesse Holland and Abram Brumbelow.
Page 168.

Thomas J. Kemp and Nancy Casey, 25 Oct. 1854, at Jas. Casey's,
by Thos. F. Bludworth, J.P. Page 168.

Huey J. Traywick and Matilda Shipes, 20 Dec. 1854, at Andrew J.
Shipes', by W. N. Adkinson. Page 169.

Joseph L. Parmer and Roxana Bush, 2 Nov. 1854, at Nancy Bush's,
by D. A. Bush, J.P. Page 169.

Allen Conant and Elizabeth Izzabel Walker, 5 Nov. 1854, by D. M.
Weston, J.P. Consent of her step-father, Hezzikiak
Wood. Page 169.

Henry W. Beauchamp and Rebecca R. Fenn, 9 Nov. 1854, at Mathew
    Fenn's, by Judge W. R. Cowen. Consent of his
    guardian, G. Beauchamp. Page 170.

James Newman and Candis Kemp, 6 Nov. 1854, by Joseph Thigpen,
    M.G. Consent of his guardian, Michael Cowen.
    Page 170.

Alfred J. Stuckey and Nancy A. E. Sheppard, 12 Nov. 1854, at
    William Sheppard's, by Aaron Helms. Consent of
    his father, Starkey Stuckey. Page 171.

James W. Cawthorn and Nancy J. Blair, 7 Nov. 1854, at Probate
    Office, by W. R. Cowen, Judge. Page 171.

Ryan Bennett and Margarett Daniel, issued 7 Nov. 1854, executed
    by Jas. Harrod, M.G. Page 172.

Henry Lawhorn and Mrs. Mary Ann Slack, 23 Nov. 1854, at Mrs.
    Slack's, by Jas. Harrod, M.G. Page 172.

Robert Alexr. Price and Miss Z. L. Helms, 23 Jan. 1853, by
    Aaron Helms. Page 172.

Patison Hagler and Nancy Thomas, 10 Feb. 1853, by Aaron Helms.
    Page 172.

Elijah Hutson and Harriet Bass, 20 Jan. 1853, by Aaron Helms.
    Page 173.

Mark C. Parker and Joanna D. Whigham, 23 Nov. 1854, by J. J.
    Dickson. Consent of her father, Joseph Thigpen.
    Page 173.

William Harper and Catherine Sauls, 26 Nov. 1854, at Hardy
    Stevens', by C. A. Parker, M.G. Page 173.

Charles Meritt and Angeline Newman, 17 Nov. 1854, at Probate
    Office, by Judge W. R. Cowen. Page 174.

Thomas J. Smith and Martha F. Slack, issued 18 Nov. 1854, return
    not recorded. Consent of parents, Samuel J. Smith
    and Mary A. Slack. Page 174.

Edward N. Moreland and Rebecca J. King, 30 Nov. 1854, at Levy
    King's, by J. J. Dickson. Consent of her parents,
    Levi and Susan A. King. Page 174.

William Barry and Martha Williams, 7 Dec. 1854, by Solomon
    Sikes, M.G. Page 175.

Joseph H. Thigpen and Nancy M. Gilchrist, 7 Dec. 1854, at Mr.
    Gilchrist's, by C. A. Parker, M.G. Page 175.

Elisha Durden and Epsey Hawkins, 7 Dec. 1854, at T. A. J.
    Hawkins', by Seaborn Jones, J.P. Page 175.

Isaiah G. Childree and Rebecca Ann Bethea, 10 Dec. 1854, at Mr.
    Bethea's, by Middleton Brooks, M.G. Page 176.

Joseph C. Green and Amanda Tamples, 14 Nov. 1854, at J. Tamples',
    by Elder Wm. Lee. Page 176.

Daniel P. Nobles and G. Lucinda Massa, 13 Dec. 1854, at Semion
        Massa's, by Thos. F. Bludworth. Page 176.

William B. Reed and Rebecca Ann Eubanks, 19 Dec. 1854, at Mrs.
        Eubanks', by W. A. McCarty, M.G. Page 177.

Lodwick M. Harrell and Nancy Temples, 24 Dec. 1854, by R. N.
        Lowe, J.P. Consent of her parents, John and
        Elizabeth Temples. Page 177.

Stephen Driggers and Artemasia Lott, 21 Dec. 1854, at Arthur
        Lott's, by L. L. Pierce, J.P. Consent of her
        father and his guardian, Arthur Lott. Page 177.

D. V. Glenn and Rebecca C. Rivers, 2 Jan. 1855, at Col. T. H.
        Rivers', by Jas. W. Shores. Page 178.

Hugh A. Nixon and Sarah J. McDonald, 24 Dec. 1854, at Glennville,
        by John Crowell, M.G. Page 178.

Mathew W. Smart and Precilla M. Tarver, 21 Dec. 1854, at Mrs.
        Tarver's, by John W. Norton. Page 178.

Thomas Halcombe and Francis E. Wellborn, 19 Dec. 1854, at Dr. B.
        Peterson's, by Wm. H. McIntosh. Page 179.

J. N. Dawkins and Lucia McDonald, 25 Dec. 1854, at Mrs. McDonald's
        by Rev. Tompson J. Glenn. Page 179.

Samuel F. Lightner and Mary T. Cotton, 21 Dec. 1854, at L.
        Gibons', by J. J. Dixon, M.G. Page 179.

James W. Stokes and Martha A. Lee, 20 Dec. 1854, at Mrs. Lee's,
        by Judge W. R. Cowen. Page 179.

John F. Davis and Effy Ann Volentine, 21 Dec. 1854, at Mathy
        Volentine's, by B. D. Loveless, M.G. Page 180.

James W. Shelby and Nancy E. Parker, 24 Dec. 1854, by J. J.
        Dixon, M.G. Consent of her father, C. A. Parker.
        Page 180.

Andrew J. McKinney and Amanda J. Bounds, issued 22 Dec. 1854,
        return not recorded. Page 181.

James M. Ethridge and Elizabeth M. Hill, 24 Dec. 1855 (issued
        23 Dec. 1854) by Z. J. Daniel, J.P. Consent of
        her father, William Hill. Page 181.

Malcom McSwean and Elizabeth Horn, 28 Dec. 1854, at Eli Horn's,
        by W. N. Adkinson, J.P. Page 181.

Alfred Laten and Nancy Williamson, 2 Jan. 1855, at Chas.
        Williams', by H. Pipkin, J.P. Page 182.

John McKinny and Martha J. Herron, 28 Dec. 1854, at D. H.
        Bishop's, by J. J. Josey, J.P. Page 182.

W. M. Graves and Jane Ziterower, issued 27 Dec. 1854, return
        not recorded. Page 183.

David Owens and Henrietta Whittington, 28 Dec. 1854, by Jas.
        Gary, J.P. Consent of her step-father, W. D.

Faison. Page 183.

Jonathan Minton and Mary Ann Cleghorn, 7 Jan. 1855, at Eufaula,
        by Jack Hardman, J.P. Page 183.

William Evans and Rebeca Pinkleton, 31 Dec. 1854, by D. A. Bush,
        J.P. Page 184.

John F. Bryan and Margarett A. White, 2 Jan. 1855, at Jake
        White's, by Thos. F. Bludworth, J.P. Page 184.

Isaiah W. Hany (Harry?) and Mary E. Crews, 4 Jan. 1855, at John
        Crews', by C. A. Parker, M.G. Page 184.

S. G. Whatley and Miss J. E. Sanders, 7 Jan. 1855, by D. A.
        Norton, J.P. Page 185.

Joel T. Teal and Marjery Johnson, 4 Jan. 1855, by T. W. Richards,
        J.P. Page 185.

George W. Gallaway and Salany E. Cooper, 4 Jan. 1855, at J. P.
        McNair's, by L. L. Pierce, J.P. Page 185.

Daniel G. Burney and Rebecca McNeal, 4 Jan. 1855, at John
        McNair's, by R. N. Low, J.P. Page 186.

Dennis F. Nolin and Maria G. Taylor, 4 Jan. 1855, at Washington
        Taylor's, by W. N. Adkinson. Page 186.

Michael W. Floyd and Dicv Benton, 7 Jan. 1855, at C. S. Warr's,
        by L. L. Pierce, J.P. Page 186.

John W. Whitton and Mary Jane Whittington, issued 11 Jan. 1855,
        return not recorded. Page 187.

Henry Hall and Elizabeth Paramore, 14 Jan. 1855, at J. Paramore's,
        by Seaborn Jones, J.P. Page 187.

Jonathan Tillman and Ziphlia E. Westbrook, 18 Jan. 1855, by
        Elder W. Lee. Page 187.

William Stokes and Mary Powell, 18 Jan. 1855, at Mrs. Powell's,
        by Miles McInnis, J.P. Page 187.

Jesse Sutton and Sarah Teal, 21 Jan. 1855, at William Teal's,
        by Miles McInnis, J.P. Page 188.

Gabrul N. King and Mary Spurlock, 21 Jan. 1855, at Solomon
        Spurlock's, by Abner Belcher. Page 188.

James Cash and Nancy Jane Ivy, 30 Jan. 1855, by Geo. W. Carter,
        M.G. Page 189.

John Perkins and Sarah Winslett, 30 Jan. 1855, at Andrew Sanders',
        by Jas. Harrod, M.G. Page 189.

John R. Siler and Mary Morrison, 18 Feb. 1855, at Mrs.
        Morrison's, by M. A. Patterson. Page 189.

Samuel King and Ann Bell, 11 Feb. 1855, by Thos. F. Bludworth,
        J.P. Page 189.

Samuel Passmore and Ann O'Bryan, 8 Feb. 1855, at Mrs. O'Bryan's, by L. L. Pierce, J.P.   Page 190.

William P. Butler and Malinda Anglin, 15 Feb. 1855, at Wm.
    Anglin's, by B. A. Barron, J.P.   Page 190.

Robert D. Thornton and Ann E. Seay, 22 Feb. 1855, by J. M.
    Thornton, J.P.   Page 190.

Britt McDonald and Ann Pournell, 21 Feb. 1855, at Eufaula, by
    Jas. L. Collins, M.G.   Page 191.

F. W. Kelly and Lizzie A. Davis, 22 Feb. 1855, at Eufaula, by
    John R. McIntosh.   Page 191.

T. N. Holleman and Sarah J. Whigham, issued 26 Feb. 1855, return
    not recorded.   Page 191.

Charles R. Walden and Susanah E. Cobb, 5 Mar. 1855, at Harriett
    W. Cobb's, by Jno. M. White.   Consent of his
    father, Green Walden, of Pulaski County, Georgia.
    Page 192.

R. T. Ranson and Mary A. Henly, 4 Mar. 1855, at Clayton, by
    G. R. Tally, M.G.   Page 192.

Benjamin G. Lewis and Basheba E. Holmes, 8 Mar. 1855, by Miles
    McInnis, J.P.   Page 192.

Z. M. L. Lewis and Jane Edge, 8 Mar. 1855, at Mrs. Edge's, by
    Elder Wm. Lee.   Page 193.

Edmund Lilly and Catherine E. Buchanon, 20 Mar. 1855, at Eufaula,
    by J. R. McIntosh.   Page 193.

William Norwood and Emma Coker, 15 Mar. 1855, by A. E. Jones,
    J.P.   Page 193.

Jesse L. Hays and Sarah Dansey, 18 Mar. 1855, at Jas. Richards',
    by T. W. Richards, J.P.   Page 194.

John Bludworth and Missouri Brewer, 27 Mar. 1855, by B. D.
    Loveless, M.G.   Consent of parents, Thos. F.
    Bludworth and James Brewer.   Page 194.

Joel D. Stokes and Elizabeth Kitcham, 8 Apr. 1855, at Mrs.
    Kitcham's, by Miles McInnis, J.P.   Page 195.

Lemuel Hargroves and Martha Virginia Clark, 5 Apr. 1855, at
    James Clark's, by Joel Sims, M.G.   Page 195.

Asa G. Thomas and Sarah Elizabeth Morrison, 7 Apr. 1855, at
    Eufaula, by J. R. McIntosh.   Page 195.

Reubin T. Sauls and Satchy Chambers, issued 17 Apr. 1855, return
    not recorded.   Page 196.

Elisha W. Harrison and Elizabeth Taylor, issued 17 Apr. 1855,
    return not recorded.   Page 196.

Burton Brown and Sarah E. Freeman, 24 Apr. 1855, at William
    Freeman's, at Glennville, by James W. Shores, M.G.
    Page 196.

Caleb W. Earp and Martha A. Johnson, 29 Apr. 1855, by C. S. Hunt,
M.G. Consent of her mother, Axey Johnson. Page
197.

Easler Kilpatrick and Mary Floyd, 19 Apr. 1855, at Mrs. Floyd's,
by Joseph Thigpen, M.G. Page 197.

Levi Dunn and Epsey Sanders, 26 Apr. 1855, at Thos. Sanders',
by D. A. Norton, J.P. Page 197.

Moses Mathews and Susan Ann Bryan, 6 May 1855, by John W. Norton.
Page 198.

Thomas G. Bass and Sarah E. Hancock, 10 May 1855, by Moses
Padgett. Consent of her father, Josiah Hancock.
Page 198.

John G. Smith and Sarah Weathers, 10 May 1855, at Wm. Weathers',
by Jno. M. White, J.P. Page 199.

John B. Massey and Mary J. Ingram, 27 May 1855, by W. B. Weston.
Consent of her father, O. C. Ingram. Page 199.

J. S. Thomas and Amantha Taylor, 24 May 1855, by J. J. Dickson,
M.G. Consent of her mother, Elizabeth Taylor.
Page 200.

Jacob R. Walters and Margarett King, 17 May 1855, by J. J.
Dickson, M.G. Consent of her father, Thomas
King. Page 200.

Lewis Miller and Elizabeth Smith, 5 June 1855, by T. W.
Richards, J.P. Page 201.

William Broach and Nancy Eidson, 28 June 1855, at Mrs. Eidson's,
by M. A. Patterson, M.G. Page 201.

John T. Carter and Caroline Parmer, 27 June 1855, at Benj.
Parmer's, by A. E. Jones, J.P. Page 201.

W. L. Hatcher and Sophrona McKinny, 1 July 1855, at Lucinda
McKinny's, by B. F. Beverly, J.P. Page 201.

John Lewis and Lydia F. Smith, 3 July 1855, by Miles McInnis,
J.P. Consent of her father, William T. Smith.
Page 202.

Green C. Beckham and Miss E. C. Yarrington, 3 July 1855, at
J. C. McNab's, by Joel Sims, M.G. Page 202.

Hosea Bailey and Mary Willaford, 10 July 1855, at W. Willaford's,
by D. A. Bush, J.P. Page 203.

James Sikes and Sarah Martin, 12 July 1855, at Mrs. Martin's,
by Soln. Sikes, D.D. Page 203.

Elias G. Hodges and Mary C. Perry, 17 July 1855, at S. C. Echols,
by Joel Sims, M.G. Page 203.

Alexander Dawkins and Nancy A. Green, 20 July 1855, at Thomas
Green's, by Elder Isaac Clayton. Page 204.

Stephen H. Bounds and Narcissa Lott, 19 July 1855, at Arthur

Lott's, by L. L. Pierce, J.P. Page 204.

Wiley Striplin and Mary Faulk, 27 July 1855, at L. Faulk's, by
        Judge W. R. Cowen. Page 204.

Isaac H. Harrell and Winney Rumley, 29 July 1855, by Elisha
        Williams, M.G. Page 205.

Francis A. Miles and Lucretia J. Faulk, 1 Aug. 1855, at Francis
        Johns', by Miles McInnis, J.P. Page 205.

John C. Carroll and Martha Ryals, 5 Aug. 1855, at Louisville,
        by B. F. Beverly, J.P. Page 205.

Jesse Norwood and Martha J. Bizzill, 5 Aug. 1855, at John B.
        James', by A. E. Jones, J.P. Page 206.

William E. McKenzie and Elizabeth Stewart, issued 8 Aug. 1855,
        return not recorded. Page 206.

James R. Cook and Margarett C. Griffin, 12 Aug. 1855, at John C.
        Griffin's, by Jas. Gary, J.P. Page 206.

R. L. Patterson and Sarah J. Bush, 12 Aug. 1855, at Nancy Bush's,
        by A. E. Jones, J.P. Page 207.

Columbus Clark and Tabitha Carr, issued 13 Aug. 1855, return not
        recorded. Page 207.

Jesse J. Taylor and Caroline Teal, 16 Aug. 1855, at Robert
        Teal's, by T. W. Richards, J.P. Page 207.

James Warren and Sarah Powell, 15 Aug. 1855, at E. A. Warren's,
        by B. A. Barron, J.P. Page 208.

James W. Mabrey and Mary Ann Calloway, 23 Aug. 1855, at Daniel
        Calloway's, by Joel Sims, M.G. Page 208.

Isham Brunson and Mary Hinson, 25 Aug. 1855, at Spring Hill,
        by J. R. Stewart, J.P. Page 208.

John Vinson and Juliette M. Broadnax, 5 Sept. 1855, at Glennville,
        by Jno. Crowell, M.G. Page 209.

Thomas M. Cooper and Rebecca A. Crew, 12 Sept. 1855, at John
        Crew's, by James Bass, M.G. Page 209.

Samuel P. Bell and Susan Ann Lawhorn, 20 Sept. 1855, at Capt.
        Ott's, by J. J. Dickson, M.G.   Page 209.

David Thomas Cole and Isabel Stinson, 10 Sept. 1855, at F. A.
        McWarters', by G. R. Scroggins. Page 210.

James C. Bass ordained at Bethel Church in Randolph County,
        Georgia, on 30 Mar. 1855. Presbytery: James C.
        Cumbie & Robert Martin. Page 210.

Samuel Robinson and Sarah Haigler, 19 Sept. 1855, at Henry
        Oppert's, by Jas. S. Baxter, J.P. Page 210.

James Casey, Sr. and Nancy Deshazo, issued 17 Sept. 1855,
        return not recorded. Page 211.

Dillard Avsett and Catherine Minshew, issued 9 Oct. 1855, return not recorded. Page 211.

Lewis G. Herring and Elizabeth Holleman, issued 16 Oct. 1855, return not recorded. Page 211.

James Robinson and Margarett A. Long, 21 Oct. 1855, at N. Long's, by Jno. M. White, J.P. Page 212.

William H. Locke and Ann J. Sylvester, 30 Oct. 1855, at Mr. Sylvester's, by A. Van Hoose. Page 212.

John T. Ivy and Elizabeth E. Tiver, 23 Oct. 1855, at Joseph Ivy's, by James Gary, J.P. Page 212.

James Parramore and Chilly Tharp, 1 Nov. 1855, at Samuel Nixon's, by Jno. G. Cowan, M.G. Page 213.

Walker Richardson and Martha E. Sanford, issued 22 Oct. 1855, return not recorded. Page 213.

W. P. Stephenson and Mary E. Sparks, issued 6 Nov. 1855, return not recorded. Consent of her father, Samuel Sparks. Page 213.

Mathew Oliver ordained at Richland Baptist Church, Green County, Georgia, on 29 Nov. 1839. Recorded 12 Nov. 1855. Joseph Holmes, E. C. T. B. Thomas & Benjamin Roberts. Page 214.

Calvin Smooth and Martha A. Bostick, 2 Dec. 1855, at Mr. Bostick's, by A. Van Hoose. Page 214.

Jackson L. Vining and Sarah G. Glover, 25 Nov. 1855, at Thomas Glover's, by Abner Belcher, M.G. Page 215.

William Ross ordained at Pleasant Hill Church in Barbour Co., 9 June 1855. Recorded 17 Nov. 1855. Presbytery: Thomas B. Slade, M.G. & Jas. C. Cumbie, M.G. Page 215.

Samuel Johnson and Narcessis Starke, 29 Nov. 1855, by B. A. Barron, J.P. Page 215.

Daniel K. Baird and Lydia A. Baker, 29 Nov. 1855, at David Smith's, by T. W. Richards, J.P. Page 215.

John W. Gillinwater and Mary Ann Smith, 20 Dec. 1855, at M. Smith's, by Jack Hardman, J.P. Page 216.

Daniel M. Marshall and Miss E. T. Lott, 4 Dec. 1855, by B. D. Loveless, M.G. Consent of his father, Thomas Marshall. Page 216.

Richard B. Lingo and Amanda M. Horn, 6 Dec. 1855, at Eli Horn's, by Rev. S. N. Graham. Consent of his father, R. T. Lingo. Page 217.

John J. Lowman and Eliza J. Sanders, 11 Dec. 1855, at Mr. Florence's, by John W. Norton. Page 217.

Enoch H. Owens and Catherine McCrackin, 13 Dec. 1855, by Jas. Gary, J.P. Consent of parents, Mrs. Owens and

Mary McCrackin. Page 217.

Wm. James Volentine and Martha E. Burlison, 16 Dec. 1855, by
B. A. Varron, J.P. Consent of her father, S. W.
Burlison. Page 218.

George F. Picket and Mary Ann Draper, 19 Dec. 1855, by Thos. F.
Bludworth, J.P. Consent of her father, Peter
Draper. Page 218.

Azor Van Hoose and Missouri F. Cotton, 18 Dec. 1855, at Z. J.
Daniel's, by E. Z. Van Hoose. Page 219.

Darling Pittman and Theodosia M. Wilder, 25 Dec. 1855, at
Louisville, by B. F. Beverly, J.P. Page 219.

Dock Curenton and Virginia Bryan, 20 Dec. 1855, at Mrs. Jas.
Bryan's, by W. Ross, M.G. Page 220.

Mack Deas and Caroline Ashley, 20 Dec. 1855, near Rocky Hill, by
Rev. G. W. Barker. Page 220.

Thomas C. Efurd and Elizabeth C. Herring, 27 Dec. 1855, at West
Herring's, by B. Williams, J.P. Page 220.

N. A. McNeil and Eliza Burlison, 30 Dec. 1855, at S. W. Burlison's
by Thos. F. Bludworth. Page 221.

David Holder and Eliza Parker, 30 Dec. 1855, at Kincion Parker's,
by Thos. F. Bludworth. Page 221.

Jarret F. Baker and Savanah J. Gibbins, issued 1 Jan. 1856,
return not recorded. Page 221.

George D. Conner and Mariah G. Upshaw, 17 Jan. 1856, at
Glennville, by Wm. A. McCarty, M.G. Page 222.

William Smith and Sarah E. Coleman, 15 Jan. 1856, at Joseph
West's, by H. Pipkin, J.P. Page 222.

Joshua McDonald and Elizabeth Martin, 10 Jan. 1856, at Sylvester
Martin's, by S. C. Bradley. Page 223.

John A. Davis and Nancy Lott, 15 Jan. 1856, by L. L. Pierce,
J.P. Page 223.

John Henly and Elizabeth Fuqua, 16 Jan. 1856, by L. L. Pierce,
J.P. Consent of her father, Sterling Fuqua.
Page 223.

Lemuel Hinson and Sarah E. Gibson, 13 Jan. 1856, by B. D.
Loveless, M.G. Page 224.

James R. J. Floyd and Martha S. Grubbs, 17 Jan. 1856, by Philip
Belcher, M.G. Consent of her parents, William
and Nancy Grubbs. Page 224.

William B. Hall and Sarah Green, 17 Jan. 1856, at Eufaula, by
John H. McIntosh. Page 225.

James Williams and Christian McCrany, 17 Jan. 1856, at Malcom
McCrany's, by Duncan McGilvary. Page 225.

Joseph G. Snead and Mary Brazel, 24 Jan. 1856, by Philip Belsher, M.G. Consent of his father, William M. Snead. Page 225.

Thomas Courson and Sarah McIntosh, 17 Jan. 1856, at Daniel McIntosh's, by Jas. Gary, J.P. Page 226.

Charles W. Hagler and Pomelia Silas, 30 Jan. 1856, at P. F. A. Posey's, by Thos. F. Bludworth. Page 226.

L. L. Armstrong and Nancy J. Hill, 7 Feb. 1856, at Felix Hill's, by G. R. Scroggins. Page 226.

Amon E. Faner and Drucilla D. Davis, 12 Feb. 1856, at Mr. Davis', by J. M. Thornton, J.P. Page 227.

Thomas C. Helms and Sarah Warren, 7 Feb. 1856, at Mrs. Warren's, by D. A. Bush, J.P. Page 227.

John M. Hughes and Eliza A. C. Walton, 14 Feb. 1856, at Glenn-Ville, by D. M. Weston, J.P. Page 227.

Thomas Day and Telitha Mayo, issued 12 Feb. 1856, return not recorded. Page 228.

William C. Jordan and Frances Thornton, 14 Feb. 1856, by F. H. Moss, M.G. Consent of her father, Reubin Thorn-ton. Page 228.

James A. Bowden and Mary A. Stewart, 14 Feb. 1856, at James Stewart's, by A. E. Jones. Page 229.

Elias Bryan and Sarah Bryan, 14 Feb. 1856, at William Bryan's, by Seaborn Jones, J.P. Page 229.

E. S. Harrel and Mary Ann Sandman, 18 Feb. 1856, at Louisville, by B. F. Beverly, J.P. Page 229.

L. V. Sheppard and Georgiann McGee, 24 Feb. 1856, at Alfred McGee's, by Abner Belcher, M.G. Page 230.

Joseph T. Smith and Sophrona Evans, 28 Feb. 1856, at Glennville, by W. Ross, M.G. Page 230.

John J. Rile and Sarah A. C. Bagget, 2 Mar. 1856, by Miles McInnis, J.P. Page 230.

John C. Storee and Anna C. Little, 9 Mar. 1856, at J. Little's, by Jos. Thigpen, M.G. Page 231.

Benjamin Morris and Roxanna Blair, 14 Mar. 1856, at William Blair's, by D. A. Bush, J.P. Page 231.

Adam Hagler and Nancy Hagler, 4 Mar. 1856, at Elizabeth Hagler's, by Thos. F. Bludworth. Page 231.

Francis Anglin and Ledona McKinny, 6 Mar. 1856, at Wm. McKinny's, by B. Williams, J.P. Page 232.

William A. Anderson and Temple Head, 6 Mar. 1856, at E. M. Evan's, by G. R. Scroggins. Page 232.

Joseph F. Chambers and Samantha Brown, 12 Mar. 1856, at David

Chambers', by E. S. Warr, J.P. Page 232.

John F. King and Louisa Ann Parker, 13 Mar. 1856, by J. J. Dickson, M.G. Consent of her father, C. A. Parker. Page 233.

James P. Lee and Sarah Ann King, 12 Mar. 1856, by J. J. Dickson, M.G. Consent of her father, Thomas King. Page 233.

William A. Cureton and Florida Flake, 20 Mar. 1856, in Eufaula, by A. Van Hoose. Page 234.

William Clark and Julia Ann Gibson, 27 Mar. 1856, at G. W. Clark's, by Jas. Gary, J.P. Page 234.

John T. Williams and Sarah Willis, 13 Apr. 1856, at Joel Willis', by Mathew Oliver, M.G. Page 235.

William J. McBride and Mary J. Glover, 30 Mar. 1856, at J. F. Glover's, by Walter H. McDonald. Page 235.

Caswell Price and Susan M. Fowler, 27 Apr. 1856, at Rama, by W. W. B. Weston. Page 235.

Thomas Hagler and Mary Mathews, 4 Apr. 1856, by H. Oppert, J.P. Page 236.

John H. Walker and Elizabeth Walker, 8 May 1856, at Barber Walker's, by Jno. D. Collins. Page 236.

Martin O'Bryan and Wineford Byrd, 11 May 1856, at Allen Byrd's, by Ezekiel Warr, J.P. Page 236.

Thomas Harris and Georgia English, 15 May 1856, at Michael Cody's, by Moses Padgett, M.G. Page 237.

John A. Jones and Martha A. Birdsong, 11 May 1856, by D. A. Bush, J.P. Page 237.

Henry D. McMillan and Amelia Francis Hightower, 20 May 1856, at Thos. A. Hightower's, by B. H. Kuser. Page 237.

L. D. Glen and Caroline Ranton, 28 May 1856, by W. N. Adkinson, J.P. Page 238.

William Booth and Jane Hagler, issued 27 May 1856, return not recorded. Page 238.

Hezekiah Smith and Harriet Shelby, 1 June 1856, by Oats Stephens, J.P. Page 238.

Jourdan Everett and Mary Jane Stedum, 1 June 1856, in Eufaula, by A. Van Hoose. Page 239.

Hartwell W. Russel and Mary F. Pope, issued 31 May 1856, executed, H. C. Russell, J.P. Page 239.

Barnabas Abbott and Sarah Roach, 3 June 1856, at Nathaniel Roach's, by Jno. M. White. Page 239.

N. B. Young and Alabama Stacy, issued 5 June 1856, return not recorded. Page 240.

Franklin Jefcoat and Nancy Ann Peacock, 12 June 1856, at Eufaula, by A. Van Hoose. Page 240.

James W. Smith and Elizabeth Verge, 15 June 1856, by B. D. Loveless, M.G. Page 240.

John Thompson and Eliza Jefcoat, 25 June 1856, at Adaline Jefcoat's, by Jack Hardman, J.P. Page 241.

John C. Moore and Miss M. V. Flournoy, 2 June 1856, at Eufaula, by Jas. L. Collins, M.G. Page 241.

J. M. Cary and Miss F. M. Gerkey, 29 June 1856, at Eufaula, by A. Van Hoose, M.G. Page 241.

F. W. Russel and Lanyann Echolds, 3 July 1856, at Clark Echolds', by H. C. Russell, J.P. Page 241.

James A. Tredwell and Martha Scott, 17 July 1856, at Eufaula, by A. Van Hoose, M.G. Page 242.

Marshall Smith and Emily A. Washburn, 14 July 1856, by M. A. Patterson, M.G. Page 242.

John Brown and Ann Cole, 3 Aug. 1856, by Oats L. Lewis, J.P. Page 242.

John Piper and Patience Spurlock, 27 July 1856, at Soln. Spurlock's, by Abner Belsher, M.G. Page 243.

Thomas W. Martin and Sarah Williams, 27 July 1856, at Daniel Williams', by D. A. Bush, J.P. Page 243.

H. D. Purswell and Amanda Vincent, 31 July 1856, by Z. Wood, J.P. Page 243.

William Smith and Elizabeth Hudson, 31 July 1856, by M. A. Patterson, M.G. Page 244.

John Miller and Emily Sheppard, 1 Aug. 1856, at Thos. Sheppard's, by Wm. Adkinson, J.P. Page 244.

William Hill and Margaret McCall, issued 5 Aug. 1856, executed, A. H. Justice, J.P. Page 244.

William Oliver and Louise Jane Norris, issued 6 Aug. 1856, return not recorded. Page 245.

Johnathan N. Smith and Lucinda Recco, 14 Aug. 1856, at W. R. Smith's, by T. W. Richards, J.P. Page 245.

W. T. J. C. Efurd and Elizabeth Bennet, 14 Aug. 1856, at Ryan Bennet's, by Buckner Williams, J.P. Page 245.

Thomas S. Lamar and Emma Perry, 21 Aug. 1856, by Wm. A. McCarty. Page 246.

Benjamin E. Stricklin and Louisa Robertson, 21 Aug. 1856, at A. Robinson's, by G. R. Scroggins, J.P. Page 246.

Thomas Owens and Jane Harp, 26 Aug. 1856, by G. W. Barker, M.G. Page 246.

Warry Killpatrick and Evey C. Cole, 31 Aug. 1856, at Warry
Killpatrick's, by G. R. Scroggins. Page 247.

Samuel A. Sims and Mary C. Best, 2 Sept. 1856, by B. H. Kuser,
J.P. Page 247.

_____ Veal and Hepsy Ann Grubbs, 11 Sept. 1856, by Wm. McCormick,
J.P. Page 247.

Isaac Hartzog and Margarett Ann M. Warr, 6 Sept. 1856, at John
Warr's, by E. S. Warr, J.P. Page 247.

Silas K. Shira and Rhoda Payne, issued 10 Sept. 1856, executed
at Jos. Payne's, by Aaron Helms. Page 248.

Samuel R. Nutt and Mildred Baker, 15 Sept. 1856, by J. J.
Harris. Page 248.

Sherrod J. Belcher and Harriet J. Richards, 30 Sept. 1856, at
Jas. Richards', by T. W. Richards, J.P. Page 248.

William McLeod and Nancy Ann Johnson, 30 Sept. 1856, at L. A. T.
Johnson's, by J. G. Tyson, M.G. Page 249.

William F. Kelly and Barbary Rutland, issued 27 Sept. 1856,
return not recorded. Page 249.

Dillan Everett and Adalan Garland, 7 Oct. 1856, at Washington
Garland's, by Seaborn Jones. Page 249.

Robert Flournoy and Susan McKenzie, 30 Sept. 1856, at D.
McKenzie's, by E. Y. Van Hoose. Page 250.

Benjamin Palmer and Mary Sloan, 1 Oct. 1856, at Mrs. Sloan's,
by Wm. McCormick, J.P. Page 250.

Augustus Glover and Winifred E. Pierce, 14 Oct. 1856, at Jesse
Pierce's, by E. S. Warr. 'Page 250.

H. D. Cumbie and Sarah Thomas, issued 15 Oct. 1856, return
not recorded. Page 251.

Thomas L. Griffin and Mary Blakey, 23 Oct. 1856, at Wm. Blakey's,
by Duncan McGilvary, J.P. Page 251.

Martin M. Hinson and Mary Albritain, 22 Oct. 1856, by B. D.
Loveless, M.G. Page 251.

Isaac Willis and Mariah Elizabeth Brown, 27 Oct. 1856, by D. A.
Bush, J.P. Page 251.

Solomon W. Vickers and Ann R. Rivers, 26 Oct. 1856, by James
Gary, J.P. Page 252.

Lewis Price and Mary Elizabeth Bowden, 30 Oct. 1856, at Jesse
B. Bowden's, by Joel Sims, M.G. Page 252.

J. W. Warr and Margarett L. Baker, 6 Nov. 1856, at Larkin
Baker's, by Ezekeal Warr, J.P. Page 252.

Joseph Abner and Mahaly Shipes, 13 Oct. 1856, at Martha Shipes',
by W. N. Adkinson, J.P. Page 253.

Elisha Jenkins and Francis C. Ball, 6 Nov. 1856, by J. J.
Dickson, M.G. Page 253.

Frank Delony and Annie Gachet, 4 Nov. 1856, by W. H. Ellison,
D.D. Page 253.

William G. Dorman and Sarah Johnson, 4 Nov. 1856, by B. D.
Loveless, M.G. Page 253.

Warren D. Jackson and Mary A. Hinson, 2 Nov. 1856, at R. W. W.
Bell's, by B. D. Loveless, M.G. Page 254.

George W. Golden and Elizabeth Williams, 9 Nov. 1856, at Mrs.
Williams', by Thos. W. Richards, J.P. Page 254.

Jonathan Abbet and Sarah Scott, 6 Nov. 1856, at Midway, by H.
Pipkin, J.P. Page 254.

John D. Lott and Miss S. J. C. Aland, 12 Nov. 1856, by A. E.
Jones, J.P. Consent of her father, Albert Aland.
Page 255.

J. E. W. Oliver and Emily Blakey, issued 12 Nov. 1856, return
not recorded. Page 255.

William T. Hightower and Julia A. Tinsley, 13 Nov. 1856, at Mrs.
Tinsley's, by Moses Padget, M.G. Page 255.

Russell Norton and Julia Ann Herring, 13 Nov. 1856, at John
Herring's, by E. Y. Van Hoose. Page 256.

Samuel Herring and Lucretia Welden, 19 Nov. 1856, by Thos. F.
Bludworth, J.P. Page 256.

Hugh McCall and Nancy Alums, 20 Nov. 1856, executed. Page 256.

Robert J. Stokes and Martha Giss, 20 Nov. 1856, executed. Page
257.

Jesse Hinson and Catharine English, 16 Nov. 1856, by B. D.
Loveless, M.G. Page 257.

John Vickers and Luvina Lee, issued 17 Nov. 1856, return not
recorded. Page 257.

Alford H. Lardwick and Amelia Ann Evans, issued 18 Nov. 1856,
return not recorded. Page 257.

John H. Patterson and Martha A. Ginwright, 18 Dec. 1856, at
Stephen Hughs', by A. E. Jones, J.P. Page 258.

Thomas J. Commander and Amanda Ann Elizabeth Hall, 25 Nov. 1856,
at John Hall's, by Jonathan G. Tyson, M.G. Page
258.

James M. Watkins and Martha Wise, 23 Nov. 1856, at Mr. Wise's,
by Thos. W. Richards. Page 258.

D. E. Corbit and Mrs. Sarah Jane Thomas, 26 Nov. 1856, at
Nicholas Zorn's, by J. S. Solomon. Page 259.

Jesse Slack and Catherine Minchew, 27 Nov. 1856, at Mr. Minchew's,
by Archibald Nobles, J.P. Page 259.

Fitz William Smith and Mary F. Alexander, 4 Dec. 1856, by A.
Van Hoose. Page 259.

Robert Bevel and Emeliza Fortner, 1 Dec. 1856, at Lewella Earp's,
by T. F. Bludworth, J.P. Page 260.

William H. Wade and Sarah Jane Wright, 8 Dec. 1856, by James
Gary, J.P. Page 260.

Absalom A. Fuqua and Charity Heron, 7 Dec. 1856, by D. McGilvary,
J.P. Page 260.

William T. Robinson and Elinnah E. Flake, 22 Dec. 1856, at
Glennville, by D. S. T. Douglas. Page 261.

Samuel Simpkins and Mary Ann Wedden, 1 Dec. 1856, by D. McNab,
J.P. Page 261.

William Baker and Molsey Miller, 14 Dec. 1856, executed at
Martin Miller's. Page 261.

James Bullard and Martha Draper, 18 Dec. 1856, by B. D.
Loveless, M.G. Page 261.

William J. Turlington and Ruth Ann Bryan, 14 Dec. 1856, at T. F.
Bryan's, by Elijah Ray, J.P. Page 262.

Alexander Benefield and Mary Ann Mayner, 14 Dec. 1856, by Z. J.
Daniel, J.P. Page 262.

Joseph Floyd and Sarah A. Butts, 17 Dec. 1856, at Chas. Butts',
by E. S. Warr, J.P. Page 262.

John D. Carden and Phebe P. Tedwell, 28 Dec. 1856, at C. D.
Tedwell's, by J. J. Dickson, M.G. Page 263.

Samuel Simpkins and Mary A. M. Whiddon, 6 Dec. 1856, by D.
McNab, J.P. Page 263.

Aaron Worthington and Adaline Cariker, 19 Dec. 1856, at M. M.
Cariker's, by Seaborn Jones, J.P. Page 263.

John Law and Mary Elizabeth Wilkison, 17 Dec. 1856, by Aaron
Helms. Page 264.

William E. Smith and May Pitman, 21 Dec. 1856, at Young Smith's,
by Soln. Sikes, M.G. Page 264.

James Wright and Jane Wright, 19 Dec. 1856, at Elizabeth
Wright's, by R. N. Lowe, J.P. Page 264.

Stephen W. Ethrage and Rachel M. Purswell, 21 Dec. 1856, by Z.
Wood, J.P. Page 265.

J. A. Sylvester and Julia A. Woods, 25 Dec. 1856, at Eufaula,
by R. C. Smith, M.G. Page 265.

J. T. Fenn and Rachel Ann Fryer, 23 Dec. 1856, by E. Y. Van
Hoose. Page 265.

John T. Crawford and Jane Tomlin, issued 23 Dec. 1856, return
not recorded. Page 265.

Thomas J. Collins and Elender Barrington, 2 Jan. 1857, by H. Oppert, J.P. Page 266.

Thomas Messeck and Mary E. Williams, 6 Jan. 1857, at Mrs. Williams', by A. H. Justice, J.P. Page 266.

John D. Belcher and Mary Grubbs, 8 Jan. 1857, at Wm. Grubbs', by B. D. Loveless, M.G. Page 266.

Campbell Stucky and Christna McLean, 9 Jan. 1857, by Soln. Sikes, D.D. Page 267.

William D. Tindall and Margaret Ann Smith, 8 Jan. 1857, at J. B. R. Smith's, by H. M. Greathouse. Page 267.

John L. Parsons and Lincy A. Worrel, 11 Jan. 1857, by D. A. Bush, J.P. Page 267.

Thomas Campbell and Rebecca A. E. Nicholds, 14 Jan. 1857, by Miles McInnis, J.P. Page 268.

Joseph T. Kenedy and Mary M. A. Williamson, 18 Jan. 1857, at Wm. Williamson's, by Robt. Toler, M.G. Page 268.

Daniel E. Bass and Mary Jane M. Beryhill, 18 Jan. 1857, at Sarah Berryhill's, by E. S. Warr, J.P. Page 268.

A. A. Crews and Sarah Jane Thomas, 18 Jan. 1857, at Jonathan Thomas', by D. McGilvary, J.P. Page 268.

Eli Jorden and Elizabeth C. Pert, 18 Jan. 1857, by Jack Hardman, J.P. Page 269.

William R. Bounds and Lydia L. Butts, 21 Jan. 1857, at Charles Butts', by E. S. Warr, J.P. Page 269.

John R. Thomas and Rebecca Franklin, 29 Jan. 1857, at T. Franklin's, by Jno. M. White, J.P. Page 269.

John Gillis, Jr. and Catharine McLean, 28 Jan. 1857, at Hugh McLean's, by Soln. Sikes, M.G. Page 270.

George H. Slaughter and May Jane Unity Lunceford, 29 Jan. 1857, at J. P. Lunceford's, by Thos. A. Hightower, J.P. Page 270.

J. C. David and Miss L. A. Garland, 3 Feb. 1857, by W. K. Norton, M.G. Page 270.

William A. Liptrot and Julia V. Faulk, 2 Feb. 1857, at L. Faulk's, by A. H. Justice, J.P. Page 271.

Jesse M. Clower and Margaret E. Boilston, 5 Feb. 1857, at A. C. Boylston's, by M. A. Patterson. Page 271.

J. W. Blakey and Caroline G. Gilchrist, 5 Feb. 1857, by J. J. Dixson, M.G. Page 271.

H. D. Williams and Sarah W. Hunt, 5 Feb. 1857, at Eufaula, by Z. J. Daniel. Page 272.

Madison C. Winslett and Elizabeth Bryan, 5 Feb. 1857, at John Bryan's, by H. C. Russell, J.P. Page 272.

John W. Stephenson and Mary E. Dillard, 10 Feb. 1857, at Edward
Dillard's, by Jno. M. White, J.P.   Page 272.

James Richardson and Mary J. Johnson, 8 Feb. 1857, by Wm. J.
Ellis, M.G.   Page 272.

Albert S. Kennedy and Nancy Ann Bowden, 19 Feb. 1857, at James
Bowden's, by Wm. W. B. Weston, M.G.   Page 273.

David Jones and Mary McDonald, 14 Feb. 1857, at Pea River Church,
by M. A. Patterson.   Page 273.

W. E. McKenzie and Elizabeth Steward, 26 Feb. 1857, at E.
Steward's, by Elder William Lee.   Page 273.

William Draper and Narcissa Riddlespurger, 18 Feb. 1857, by
B. D. Loveless, M.G.   Page 274.

John R. Burke and Susan M. Hughs, 22 Feb. 1857, by B. H. Kiezer,
J.P.   Page 274.

John Roundtree and Margaret Minshew, 26 Feb. 1857, by A. H.
Justice, J.P.   Page 274.

Samuel Griffin and Ruthy Blakey, 5 Mar. 1857, at William
Blakey's, by Joel Sims, M.G.   Page 275.

James S. Baxter and Margaret Cameron, 5 Mar. 1857, at Paul
McCall's, by Miles McInnis, J.P.   Page 275.

W. H. David and Miss E. J. Garland, 3 Mar. 1857, by William
K. Norton, M.G.   Page 275.

Floyd Martin and Elizabeth Gunnels, 5 Mar. 1857, by R. M. Lowe,
J.P.   Page 275.

John Sloan and Nancy A. Faulk, 17 Mar. 1857, at Mrs. Nancy
Faulk's, by Aaron Helms.   Page 276.

Winston Andrews and Flourida Adams, 19 Mar. 1857, by Miles
McInnis, J.P.   Page 276.

Dr. J. D. Bass and Miss F. A. Palmer, 2 Apr. 1857, at Martha
Palmer's, by F. H. Moss.   Page 276.

Sheppard W. King and Antonette Ford, 26 Mar. 1857, at W. G.
Ford's, by J. J. Dixon, M.G.   Page 277.

Elias Dowling and Elizabeth Steward, 31 Mar. 1857, at Elias
Dowling's, by Jas. Harrod, M.G.   Page 277.

Elijah Nolin and Ann Wright, 16 Apr. 1857, by D. A. Bush, J.P.
Page 277.

James Mulaney and Lucinda Stuart, 2 June 1857, at T. Williams',
by Elder William Lee.   Page 278.

James F. Tate and Sarah Hall, 12 Apr. 1857, at Sarah Tate's,
by A. E. Jones, J.P.   Page 278.

Foster J. Mims and Laura E. Hancock, 19 Apr. 1857, at Mr.
Hancock's, by C. A. Parker, M.G.   Page 278.

Freeman W. Reese and Elizabeth Baker, 3 May 1857, by H. Pipkin, J.P.   Page 279.

Robert E. Ward and Lucinda Bush, 19 May 1857, at Johnathan Thomas', by Duncan McGilvary.   Page 279.

E. J. Corbit and Miss A. J. Creel, 20 May 1857, at Wm. Creel's, by Duncan McGilvary, J.P.   Page 279.

M. D. Britt and Francis Vissels, 17 May 1857, by J. J. Dickson, M.G.   Page 279.

William T. Warr and Elizabeth Butts, 28 May 1857, at Soln. Butts', by E. S. Warr, J.P.   Page 380.

John Powell and Edey Everett, 21 May 1857, at Eufaula, by Jack Hardman, J.P.   Page 380.

William A. Wingate and Syntha Mariah Chambers, 21 May 1857, at J. D. Chambers', by E. S. Warr, J.P.   Page 380.

John Godwin and Drusilla Pate, issued 24 May 1857, return not recorded.   Page 381.

James M. Turman and Martha Pruitt, 3 June 1857, at Jas. Pruitt's, by F. H. Moss, M.G.   Page 381.

Eli Herring and Eliza Ann Kent, issued 29 May 1857, executed at Aaron Kent's, by C. S. Pelham.   Page 381.

Ervin Green and Catherine McMilan, issued 30 May 1857, return not recorded.   Page 382.

Lovick P. Allen and Ann Augustus Coleman, 23 June 1857, at Mrs. Coleman's, by Robt. Keith, M.G.   Page 382.

John W. Lewis and Allice West, 19 June 1857, by Young Wood, J.P.   Page 382.

Peter Joiner and May Jane Bostick, 24 June 1857, at Mr. Bostick's, by B. T. C. Banks.   Page 382.

Paul McCall and Harrit McRae, 2 July 1857, at Jno. E. McRae's, by M. A. Patterson.   Page 383.

Isaac Messick and Mary E. Roundtree, 2 July 1857, at Mrs. Roundtree's, by A. H. Justice, J.P.   Page 383.

Archibald Nobles and Nancy Ann Murry, 5 July 1857, at Thos. E. Hix's, by Jack Hardman, J.P.   Page 383.

A. M. Marshall and Adalaid Lott, 12 July 1857, at Mrs. Lott's, by Seaborn Jones, J.P.   Page 384.

W. W. Hamilton and Amelia Odum, 9 July 1857, at J. C. McNab's, by E. Y. Van Hoose.   Page 384.

Thomas H. Anglian and Caroline Boilston, 14 July 1857, at J. P. Boilston's, by Aaron Helms.   Page 385.

J. D. Bush and Sarah Ann McDonald, issued 11 July 1857, return not recorded.   Page 385.

James B. Davis and Obedience Spurlock, issued 18 July 1857,
     return not recorded. Page 385.

Samuel F. Smith and Mary Jane Barker, 22 July 1857, by J. S.
     Williams, Judge of Probate. Page 386.

Stephen B. Lewis and Mary E. Beasley, 30 July 1857, at Mrs.
     Beasley's, by Soln. Sikes, D.D. Page 386.

Maxamillian B. Wellborn and Emma J. Dent, 5 July 1857, at J. H.
     Dent's, by Judge J. S. Williams. Page 386.

J. E. Johnson and Levina Miller, 4 Aug. 1857, at Geo. Miller's,
     by Jas. A. Scarborough. Page 387.

B. S. Lunsford and Sarah Ann E. Sasser, 29 July 1857, at Clayton,
     by Judge J. S. Williams. Consent of her guardian,
     George W. Coleman. Page 387.

J. D. Bostick and Nicy Permelia Ann Napper, 6 Aug. 1857, by G. C.
     Efurd, J.P. Consent of his father, John W. J.
     Bostick. Page 387.

John W. Berry and Lydia Ann E. Martin, 9 Aug. 1857, by Elijah
     Ray, J.P. Page 388.

W. A. Russel and Sallie E. Lamar, 12 Nov. 1857, at Glennville,
     by W. K. Norton, M.G. Page 388.

W. H. Harrell and Miss S. A. Craig, 13 Aug. 1857, at Jacob
     Harrell's, by T. S. Glenn, M.G. Page 388.

John Butler and Susan Alford, 13 Aug. 1857, at Wm. P. Butler's,
     by R. N. Lowe, J.P. Page 389.

William M. Lamkin and Mary Jane Oliver, 16 Aug. 1857, at Enon,
     by W. H. Ellison, D.D. Page 389.

Christopher Teal and Diga Sutton, 20 Aug. 1857, at Jesse
     Sutton's, by Miles McInnis, J.P. Page 389.

Gilford Kent and Mary T. Steward, 20 Aug. 1857, at Jas.
     Steward's, by D. A. Bush, J.P. Page 390.

Z. F. Colly and Mary A. E. Glover, 26 Aug. 1857, by E. Y. Van
     Hoose. Consent of her father, H. G. Glover. Page
     390.

Benjamin Franklin Stuckey and Jemima Little, 13 Sept. 1857, at
     J. Little's, by Judge J. S. Williams. Page 390.

William Baker and Elizabeth Warr, 6 Sept. 1857, at J. T. Warr's,
     by E. S. Warr, J.P. Page 391.

Andrew Bass and Elender Davis, 13 Sept. 1857, at John Davis',
     by Rev. John D. Collins. Page 391.

James P. Little and Ellender Brown, 17 Sept. 1857, at Jesse
     Brown's, by Thos. A. Hightower. Page 392.

William M. Tilly and Elizabeth Brown, 20 Sept. 1857, at Chas. A.
     Brown's, by Thos. A. Hightower. Page 392.

Thomas Barnes and Elizabeth Evans, 1 Oct. 1857, at William
        Evans', by R. N. Lowe. Page 392.

James Griffin and Sarah Justice, 1 Oct. 1857, at Mrs. Sarah
        Picket's, by J. J. Dickson. Page 392.

Mathew Lasiter and Mary Parmer, 24 Sept. 1857, at Mary Parmer's,
        by A. E. Jones, J.P. Page 393.

William G. Johnson and Jane Campbell, 24 Sept. 1857, at R.
        Johnson's, by A. H. Justice, J.P. Page 393.

William A. Oliver and Malinda Bsss, 28 Sept. 1857, at Samuel
        Wilkinson's, by Jno. D. Collins. Page 393.

William F. Baley and Sarah A. Taylor, 26 Sept. 1857, at Redin
        Taylor's, by A. E. Jones, J.P. Page 394.

James Cash and Abi King, 27 Sept. 1857, at Midway, by Wm. A.
        McCarty, M.G. Page 394.

J. S. Killpatrick and Sarah Ann Little, 28 Sept. 1857, at Josiah
        Little's, by Robt. Toler, M.G. Page 394.

Joseph Danner and Edny Williams, 1 Oct. 1857, at Mrs. Nichols,
        by J. Danner, M.G. Page 395.

George W. Creal and Penelope A. Martin, 8 Oct. 1857, at Mrs.
        Martin's, by Soln. Sikes, M.G. Page 395.

Charles B. Gachet and Mary J. Mourton, issued 12 Oct. 1857,
        return not recorded. Page 395.

James W. Danner and Mary Bizzell, 15 Oct. 1857, at Mary
        Bizzell's, by A. H. Justice, J.P. Page 395.

John F. Cameron and Miss M. R. Pipkin, 15 Oct. 1857, at H.
        Pipkin's, by Oliver Flemming, M.G. Page 396.

Jason Cargill and Mary Kennedy, 13 Oct. 1857, at Clayton, by
        B. Williams, J.P. Page 396.

William Allen and Jane Adella Owens, 15 Oct. 1857, at Glennville,
        by John Crowell, M.G. Page 397.

John W. Brown and Frederica Conner, 15 Oct. 1857, at W. L.
        Kenndy's, by Jas. G. Tison, M.G. Page 397.

William C. Bostick and Lillian McRae, 22 Oct. 1857, at F. A.
        McRae's, by M. A. Patterson, M.G. Page 397.

Lazarus Silas and Emily Weathers, 20 Oct. 1857, at Wm. Weathers',
        by Thos. Lochla, J.P. Page 398.

Anderson W. Miller and Sarah McCarrel, 22 Oct. 1857, at P.
        McCarrell's, by Jas. A. Scarborough. Page 398.

C. H. Perry and Miss E. C. Willard, 28 Oct. 1857, at Eufaula,
        by A. Van Hoose, M.G. Page 398.

Jacob Gillmore and Mary E. Cox, 29 Oct. 1857, at Caleb Cox's,
        by Elder Wm. Lee. Page 399.

David Johnson and Haney Ann Creech, 30 Oct. 1857, at Joseph
Lindsey's, by Jas. A. Scarborough. Page 399.

E. Y. Van Hoose and Sarah A. Stringer, 29 Oct. 1857, at Clayton,
by A. Van Hoose, M.G. Page 399.

William H. Lang and Francis A. Herring, issued 5 Nov. 1857,
executed at F. A. Hearn's, by Seaborn Jones, J.P.
Page 400.

Benjamin L. Dowling and Searry D. West, 7 Nov. 1857, at J. S.
Williams', by J. S. Williams, Judge. Page 400.

Martin L. Aikins and Missouri Commander, 14 Nov. 1857, at
Newtopar, by A. H. Justice, J.P. Page 400.

Theophilus J. Robinson and Jane M. Lowe, 12 Nov. 1857, at R. N.
Lowe's, by G. R. Scroggins. Page 401.

John Bullock and Mary Amons, 11 Nov. 1857, by A. E. Jones, J.P.
Page 401.

Allen J. Rouse and Julia A. Boyleston, 10 Nov. 1857, at Clayton,
by C. A. Parker, M.G. Page 401.

William J. Martin and Christian M. A. Williams, 12 Nov. 1857,
at Martin Miller's, by Philip Belcher, M.G. Page
401.

Thomas H. Davis and Louise C. Copeland, 17 Nov. 1857, at Isaac
Copeland's, by W. M. Davis, M.G. Page 402.

A. J. Holliman and Margaret C. Whigham, 18 Nov. 1857, by Aaron
Helms, M.G. Page 402.

Charles H. Spencer and Mary S. Buckly, 18 Nov. 1857, at A. J.
Neily's, by Seaborn Jones, J.P. Page 403.

George Newman and Sarah A. Lee, 19 Nov. 1857, at Mrs. Lee's,
by H. L. Seller, L.D. Page 403.

James T. Robinson and Lavinia McKinney, 30 Nov. 1857, at
Drucilla McKinney's, by Seaborn Jones. Page 403.

Welborn J. Reaves and Mary A. Williams, 2 Dec. 1857, at Wm.
Williams', by D. McGilvary, J.P. Page 404.

James M. Mosely and Sallie A. Coleman, 3 Dec. 1857, at Glennville, by D. S. T. Douglass. Page 404.

John Forehand and Elizabeth Brooks, 3 Dec. 1857, at Stephen
Forehand's, by A. E. Jones, J.P. Page 404.

Samuel E. Mays and Catherine E. Moseley, 3 Dec. 1857, at Glennville, by D. S. T. Douglass. Page 405.

Daniel B. Easterling and Margaret Teal, 8 Dec. 1857, at Daniel
B. Teal's, by Miles McInnis. Page 405.

Marion Bates and Marietta Barnes, 10 Dec. 1857, at Myrann
Barnes', by Robt. Toler, M.G. Page 405.

Benjamin F. Wells and Martha E. Green, issued 8 Dec. 1857,

return not recorded. Page 406.

W. B. W. Lee and Louisa Jane Pierce, 10 Dec. 1857, at Lovard
Lee's, by E. S. Warr, J.P. Page 406.

J. B. Young and Emily Jones, 9 Dec. 1857, at W. W. Wilks', by
Elder Wm. Lee. Page 406.

John G. Barr and Francena E. Salles, 13 Dec. 1857, at Jas.
Bonds', by Jas. A. Scarborough. Page 407.

S. H. Gunter and Miss P. A. T. King, 15 Dec. 1857, at Reubin
Allison's, by G. W. Crymes. Page 407.

D. J. Deffnal and Caroline Marshall, 17 Dec. 1857, by R. E.
Brown. Page 407.

James S. Johnston and Catherine Delilah Padgett, 17 Dec. 1857,
at Elijah Padgett's, by G. H. Scroggins. Page
408.

John Aversett and Nancy S. L. Miles, 24 Dec. 1857, at Mr. Miles',
by Jno. Crowell, M.G. Page 408.

John Flewellen Thomas and Lavina C. Scroggins, issued 17 Dec.
1857, return not recorded. Page 408.

Snowdon T. Scroggins and Mary Ann Thomas, issued 17 Dec. 1857,
return not recorded. Page 409.

Willis Bass and Drusilley Tew, 23 Dec. 1857, at Allen Tew's,
by E. S. Warr, J.P. Page 409.

Thomas McKenna and Martha A. R. W. Booth, 22 Dec. 1857, by A. S.
Andrews, M.G. Page 409.

S. L. Scott and Tabitha M. Bryan, 24 Dec. 1857, by James Gary,
J.P. Page 410.

Thomas G. Howell and Frankey A. Payne, 22 Dec. 1857, at Joseph
Payne's, by C. S. Pelham, M.G. Page 410.

Yelverton L. Barnes and Adaline Fry, 24 Dec. 1857, at Soln.
Spurlock's, by Jack Hardman, J.P. Page 410.

Jesse Robinson and Susan M. Cowart, 23 Dec. 1857, at Eufaula,
by E. Y. Van Hoose. Page 411.

Thomas L. Holly and Mary E. Zorne, 24 Dec. 1857, at Nicholas
Zorne's, by Soln. Sikes, M.G. Page 411.

Shadrock Ethridge and Lydiann Smith, 30 Dec. 1857, at E. Smith's,
by Phillip Belcher, M.G. Page 411.

Willson Smart and Georgiann Warren, 29 Dec. 1857, at Mrs.
Warren's, by E. Y. Van Hoose. Page 411.

Archibald P. McLeod and Louisa A. Johnson, 30 Dec. 1857, at Mrs.
Johnson's, by C. A. Parker, M.G. Page 412.

William A. Barnes and Margaret R. A. Gilmore, issued 31 Dec.
1857, return not recorded. Page 412.

James Grubbs and Martha Minchew, 7 Jan. 1858, at John Minchew's,
by A. H. Justice, J.P. Page 412.

Thomas Coker and Jane Martin, 6 Jan. 1858, at Sarah Martin's,
by A. E. Jones, J.P. Page 413.

D. W. Story and Margaret A. Hays, 12 Jan. 1858, at Jas. M.
Hays', by Elder William Lee. Page 413.

Edmond M. Walker and Sarah E. Daniel, 13 Jan. 1858, at Glennville,
by J. W. Glenn, M.G. Page 413.

Benjamin Powell and Margaret Powell, 12 Jan. 1858, at Ransom
Powel's, by A. H. Justice, J.P. Page 414.

Thomas Loflin and Eliza Vining, 12 Jan. 1858, at Ashly Vinson's,
by Thos. Lockla, J.P. Page 414.

William Farmer and Rachel A. Snell, 21 Jan. 1858, at Nathaniel
Snell's, by D. McGilvary, J.P. Page 414.

John B. Davis and Sarah Homes, 21 Jan. 1858, at William Homes',
by Z. Wood, J.P. Page 415.

Moses Smith and Nancy Miller, 18 Jan. 1858, at Martin Miller's,
by Phillip Belcher, M.G. Page 415.

John W. Riley and Amanda Crabtree, 31 Jan. 1858, executed.
Page 415.

John A. Grant and Laura Russel, 27 Jan. 1858, at Jos. C.
Russel's, by C. A. Parker, M.G. Page 415.

James M. Vickers and Mary Jane Harod, 28 Jan. 1858, at Jas.
Harrod's, by Robt. W. Turner. Page 416.

John P. Dubose and Sarah A. E. Parmer, 28 Jan. 1858, at Richard
Sikes', by A. E. Jones, J.P. Page 416.

John B. Cheek and Miss N. A. Vickers, issued 28 Jan. 1858,
return not recorded. Page 416.

Elisha H. Cheek and Miss C. A. E. Martin, issued 28 Jan. 1858,
return not recorded. Page 417.

J. C. Borders and Susan M. Warren, 2 Feb. 1858, at Thos. Helms',
by O. S. Lewis, J.P. Page 417.

John H. Bates and Louisa E. Scott, 7 Feb. 1858, at Jas. Ross',
by Oliver Fleming, M.G. Page 417.

M. W. Deshazo and Amanda A. Brown, 11 Feb. 1858, at J. P.
Brown's, by D. A. Bush, J.P. Page 417.

A. H. Henley and Martha Johnson, 14 Feb. 1858, at Philip
Johnson's, by Thos. H. Hightower. Page 418.

W. B. Morrison and Sarah C. Kaigler, 17 Feb. 1858, at Reubin
Kaigler's, by J. S. Williams, Judge. Page 418.

Stephen Forehand and Jane Brown, 17 Feb. 1858, at Stephen
Forehand's, by D. A. Bush, J.P. Page 418.

Thomas Ligget and Elizabeth W. Hatcher, issued 17 Feb. 1858,
        return not recorded.   Page 419.

Benjamin Brook and Martha Ann Chambers, 18 Feb. 1858, at J. H.
        Chambers', by W. McCormick, J.P.   Page 419.

William Glass and Lucinda Miller, 18 Feb. 1858, at Mrs. Miller's,
        by Z. Wood, J.P.   Page 419.

William H. C. Gibson and Sarah E. Gamman, 18 Feb. 1858, at
        Clayton, by S. F. Lightner, J.P.   Page 420.

John Wilson and Mary Williams, 27 Feb. 1858, by Z. Wood, J.P.
        Page 420.

James Right and Sarah Streeter, issued 27 Feb. 1858, executed at
        R. Streeter's, by T. C. V. Walkey.   Page 420.

James M. Robinson and Martha L. Newman, issued 2 Mar. 1858,
        executed, Jas. A. Scarborough.   Page 421.

Samuel Bennet and Elizabeth McLean, 11 Mar. 1858, at Eufaula,
        by E. McNair, M.G.   Page 421.

Warren S. Owens and Mary Jane McCall, 20 Mar. 1858, at Louisville,
        by G. C. Efurd, J.P.   Page 421.

Nathan E. Smith and Louisa Smith, 20 Mar. 1858, by A. Grantham.
        Page 421.

Isaac M. Brooks and Caroline Wilkinson, 25 Mar. 1858, at Noah
        Wilkinson's, by Oates S. Lewis, J.P.   Page 422.

George W. Hughey and Charlotte R. McNab, 25 Mar. 1858, at
        Duncan McNab's, by L. P. Golson, M.G.   Page 422.

Shearman B. Everett and Miss H. A. Rouse, 30 Mar. 1858, at
        Clayton, by E. Y. Van Hoose, P.G.   Page 422.

Charles Butts and Miss S. A. M. Flournoy, 1 Apr. 1858, at Chas.
        Butts', by E. S. Warr, J.P.   Page 423.

G. W. W. Haley and Caroline Grant, 8 Apr. 1858, at Jno. A.
        Grant's, by B. Williams, J.P.   Page 423.

W. B. Brannon and Miss M. A. Kaigler, 15 Apr. 1858, by Wm. M.
        Motley, M.G.   Page 423.

Meritt Hix and Miss M. A. P. Skinner, 15 April 1858, by J. D.
        Collins.   Page 424.

Herman Toler and Nancy Jenkins, issued 20 Apr. 1858, executed
        by Thomas Guice, M.G.   Page 424.

W. K. P. Russel and Frances Tinsly, 22 Apr. 1858, by Thos. A.
        Hightower, J.P.   Page 424.

J. A. Miles and Mary A. E. Ludlum, 4 May 1858, at Mrs. Passmore's,
        by G. C. Efurd, J.P.   Page 425.

C. A. Malleroy and Miss F. A. Hill, 8 May 1858, at William
        Hill's, by Jno. M. White, J.P.   Page 425.

J. L. Dickinson and Sarah F. McLean, 11 May 1858, at Eufaula, by A. Van Hoose, M.G. Consent of her father, D. McLean. Page 425.

Andrew P. Johnson and Mary A. M. Russel, 20 May 1858, at Joseph C. Russell's, by B. Williams. Page 426.

Allen Byrd and Sarah Buts, 20 May 1858, by E. S. Warr, J.P. Page 426.

John L. Cooper and Margaret A. Crew, 20 May 1858, at Mrs. Crew's, by Thos. Guice. M.G. Page 427.

James Pettygrew and Caroline Thornton, 17 June 1858, at W. W. Thornton's, by Junius Jordan, M.G. Page 427.

A. L. Barkley and Miss H. O. Snipes, 7 June 1858, at Eufaula, by (illegible), minister. Page 427.

John J. Watson and Ann Rebecca Murphy, 15 June 1858, by E. C. N. Ford, J.P. Page 427.

J. P. Yarrington and H. Anna Screws, 15 June 1858, at Clayton, by D. S. T. Douglass, M.G. Page 428.

James M. Davis and Emeline Padgett, 17 June 1858, at Elijah Padgett's, by G. R. Scroggins, J.P. Page 428.

Thomas H. Stringer and Sophia T. Reed, 20 June 1858, by Jas. G. Tison, M.G. Page 429.

John B. Sears and Mary Cariker, 20 June 1858, at Mrs. Cariker's, by Judge J. S. Williams. Page 429.

George Pitman Jones and Mary A. Moffett, 23 June 1858, at Mrs. Moffett's, by E. Y. Van Hoose. Page 429.

Abram Morris and Mary Farmer, 24 June 1858, by Solomon Sikes, D.D. Page 430.

Joseph Dawson and Eliza Ann Greathouse, 26 June 1858, at John Dawson's, by Jas. A. Scarborough. Page 430.

John Mooneham and Rebecca Easterling, 1 July 1858, at Daniel B. Easterling's, by J. S. Williams. Page 431.

J. C. Lee and Miss M. E. Graves, 14 July 1858, at Glennville, by Wm. A. McCarty, M.G. Page 431.

George L. Shipman and Eliza A. E. McBride, 15 July 1858, at E. P. Wood's, by Miles McInnis, J.P. Page 431.

Stephen Herring and Caroline E. Turner, 15 July 1858, at Noel W. Turner's, by B. Williams, J.P. Page 432.

John W. Crocker and Francis S. Butts, 15 July 1858, at Solomon Butts', by E. S. Warr, J.P. Consent of parents, Cary Crocker and Solomon and Sally Butts. Page 432.

J. L. Foster and Martha A. Roundtree, 18 July 1858, by Green Malone. Page 433.

John Wesley Thurman and Mary Gene Hix, 27 Aug. 1858, by Rev.
John D. Collins. Page 433.

Green G. Thornton and Martha Pipkin, 17 July 1858, at H. Pipkin's,
by H. Pipkin, J.P. Page 433.

S. D. P. Glover and Narcessy L. Fowler, 29 July 1858, by Elijah
Ray, J.P. Page 434.

Geo. J. Turner and Miss S. A. F. Blackstock, 8 Aug. 1858, at
Mrs. E. Blackstock's, by Jas. N. Owens. Page 434.

Thomas Glass and Elizabeth Glass, 5 Aug. 1858, at L. D. Glass',
by Elijah Ray, J.P. Page 434.

Stephen T. Aplin and Tabitha Scroggins, 12 Aug. 1858, at Mr.
Scroggins', by J. J. Phillips, M.G. Page 435.

D. G. W. Warrick and Martha Minshew, 12 Aug. 1858, at Nathan
Minshew's, by A. H. Justice, J.P. Page 435.

Emanuel McNeice and Mary E. Bryan, 19 Aug. 1858, at Theophilus
Bryan's, by Thomas Lockala. Page 435.

Elias Lewis and Harriet Kilpatrick, 19 Aug. 1858, at W. H.
Kilpatrick's, by D. A. Bush, J.P. Page 436.

Comedore P. Long and Amanda C. Wilson, 26 Aug. 1858, at Archilles
Wilson's, by Jas. Gary, J.P. Page 436.

John G. Windham and Savannah Campbell, 30 Aug. 1858, at Abner
Campbell's, by A. H. Justice, J.P. Page 436.

Henry Forehand and Martha Nicholls, 2 Sept. 1858, at Clayton,
by Judge J. S. Williams. Page 437.

G. W. Raley and Priscella Herring, 6 Sept. 1858, at Mrs. Herring's
by G. C. Efurd, J.P. Page 437.

Hughey W. Glanton and Georgiann C. Horn, 29 Sept. 1858, at Eli
Horn's, by W. N. Adkinson, J.P. Page 437.

A. W. Cain and Mary Jane Grubbs, 26 Sept. 1858, at W. J.
Grubbs', by G. C. Efurd, J.P. Page 438.

Robert A. Fleming and Laura J. Cowan, 22 Sept. 1858, at
Eufaula, by E. McNair. Page 438.

Daniel McLendon and Francis A. A. Sanderman, 26 Sept. 1858, at
Nancy Hicks', by W. N. Adkinson, J.P. Page 438.

James A. B. Irvin and Virginia H. Stovall, 26 Sept. 1858, at
L. Stovall's, by Eli N. Ford, J.P. Page 439.

Malcom McGilvary and Cytha Reaves, 30 Sept. 1858, at Asher
Reaves', by D. McGilvary, J.P. Page 439.

Hobbs Bradley and Lucy Ann McKessack, 7 Oct. 1858, at Alen
McRae's, by L. P. Golson, M.G. Page 439.

William Carroll and Elizabeth Jane Marley, 13 Oct. 1858, at
H. J. Marley's, by E. S. Warr, J.P. Page 440.

Elijah T. Summers and Nancy Dean, 10 Oct. 1858, at J. G.
Beasles', by G. C. Efurd. Page 440.

L. E. Stafford and Elizabeth A. Faulk, 17 Oct. 1858, at Henry
Faulk's, by G. C. Efurd, J.P. Page 440.

B. B. McKenzie and Miss C. E. Flournoy, 14 Oct. 1858, by W. M.
Motley. Page 440.

Dennis Condry and Sarah Thomas, 14 Oct. 1858, at J. Thomas',
by D. McGilvary, J.P. Page 441.

Thomas J. Coleman and Mary V. Tarver, 21 Oct. 1858, at M. Day's,
by E. Y. Van Hoose, M.G. Page 441.

Larkin W. Powell and Martha Ann Hailey, 23 Nov. 1858, by E. Y.
Van Hoose. Page 441.

Sherman N. Cox and Elizabeth Josephine Story, 10 Nov. 1858, at
F. M. Boyd's, by Wm. Lee. Page 442.

Riley Baxley and Lincy Helms, 21 Oct. 1858, at Hilyard Helms',
by Aaron Helms, M.G. Page 442.

James S. Paulin and Ann H. Brannon, 23 Oct. 1858, at Capt.
Brannon's, by A. Van Hoose. Page 442.

George Terk and Ella McInney, 27 Oct. 1858, at Glennville, by
Jno. Crowell, M.G. Page 443.

Eli Stewart and Jane Warren, 28 Oct. 1858, at C. M. Warren's,
by J. A. Scarborough, J.P. Consent of his
mother, Elizabeth Dowlin. Page 443.

Thomas Cook and Mary Ann Cole, 4 Nov. 1858, at J. S. Cole's,
by G. R. Scroggins. Page 443.

Norman Norton and Mary A. Beasley, 4 Nov. 1858, at Jno. G.
Beasley's, by G. C. Efurd, J.P. Page 444.

John D. Kennedy and Elizabeth J. Coleman, 4 Nov. 1858, at
William Coleman's, by Wm. Ross. Page 444.

Jeremiah T. Bunting and Mrs. Jane Watson, 4 Nov. 1858, at Soln.
Spurlock's, by Z. J. Daniel. Page 444.

John Veal and Lucy Jane Patterson, 4 Nov. 1858, at Eufaula,
by E. McNair. Page 445.

Isham Jenkins and Martha Emerson, 2ᵒ Nov. 1858, at B. H.
Emerson's, by Elder William Lee. Page 445.

William Right and Amanda Herrin, 9 Nov. 1858, by Oats S.
Lewis, J.P. Page 445.

J. F. Harrison and Jane Lee, 10 Nov. 1858, at Mrs. Lee's, by
L. P. Golson, M.G. Page 446.

William A. McTyere and Terese W. Hunter, 16 Nov. 1858, at
Eufaula, by Evander McNair. Page 446.

George W. Williams and Adaline Collins, 16 Nov. 1858, at
Buckner Williams', by Judge J.S. Williams. Page 446.

Thomas R. Coleman and Mrs. Sallie A. Ott, 24 Nov. 1858, at
J. M. Spurlock's, by Green Malone, M.G. Page 446.

Daniel S. Walker and Sarah Jane Carroll, 24 Nov. 1858, at Jno.
Carroll's, by Judge J. S. Williams. Page 447.

J. M. Calhoun and Mary Thomas, 7 Dec. 1858, at Johnathan
Thomas', by D. A. Bush, J.P. Page 447.

William C. Bryan and Obedience Spurlock, 28 Nov. 1858, at
Solomon Spurlock's, by Abner Belcher. Page 448.

C. A. Cox and Mary Parker, 28 Nov. 1858, at S. Parker's, by
M. Brooks, M.G. Page 448.

Daniel M. Gannon and Mary Jane Hightower, 1 Dec. 1858, at T. A.
Hightower's, by Jno. L. Oliver, M.G. Page 448.

H. B. Hill and Jane Porter, 2 Dec. 1858, at Eufaula, by Evander
McNair. Page 449.

George Washington Gilmore and Melissa R. P. Stokes, 3 Dec.
1585, by A. E. Jones, J.P. Page 449.

Malcom McInnis and Marion Shaw, 23 Dec. 1858, at William Shaw's,
by A. H. Justice, J.P. Page 449.

W. G. Drake and Victoria A. Turner, 8 Dec. 1858, at Dr.
Turner's, by Wm. H. Ellison, D.D. Page 450.

Howell T. Eley and Mary Abney, 15 Dec. 1858, at William Abney's,
by Green Malone, M.G. Page 450.

B. F. Patterson and Eliza E. Myers, 12 Dec. 1858, at Mrs.
Myers', by R. N. Lowe, J.P. Page 450.

Eli Edge and Elizabeth Chambers, 15 Dec. 1858, at L. D.
Chambers', by E. S. Warr, J.P. Page 451.

M. K. Shelby and Addeline Warren, 14 Dec. 1858, by Judge T. S.
Williams. Consent of her guardian, Thomas E.
Warren. Page 451.

David W. Johnson and Martha A. Persons, 16 Dec. 1858, at
Glennville, by Jno. Crowell, M.G. Page 451.

Thomas S. Moffitt and Miss R. J. Herrod, 16 Dec. 1858, at Mrs.
Herrod's, by D. A. Bush, J.P. Page 452.

Thomas A. Hightower and Rachael M. Russell, 16 Dec. 1858, by
Jno. L. Oliver, M.G. Page 452.

John Deloach and Susan Carrel, 19 Dec. 1858, at Thomas Carrel's,
by A. H. Justice, J.P. Page 452.

William T. Williams and Amanda Hansford, 30 Dec. 1858, at E. R.
Flewellen's, by Jno. Crowell, M.G. Page 453.

F. M. Wood and Sarah Roquemore, 21 Dec. 1858, at Z. Roquemore's,
by L. P. Golson, M.G. Page 453.

L. P. M. Davis and Miss S. A. E. Lowman, 23 Dec. 1858, at Wm.
Lowman's, by Phillip Belcher, M.G. Page 453.

E. N. Brown and Miss F. E. Long, 28 Dec. 1858, at N. W. Long's, by E. Y. Van Hoose. Page 454.

B. C. Bennett and Amanda Huey, 28 Dec. 1858, at Adam Grubbs', by G. E. Efurd, J.P. Page 454.

Jesse Peacock and Nancy H. Daniel, 28 Dec. 1858, at Allen Daniel's, by A. H. Justice, J.P. Page 454.

John P. Scott and Mary E. Sterns, 29 Dec. 1858, by John M. White, J.P. Page 455.

Jeremiah Martin and Mary A. Vincent, 29 Dec. 1858, by Phillip Belcher, M.G. Page 455.

Thomas C. Parker and Martha C. Faulk, 30 Dec. 1858, at Lorenzo Faulk's, by H. Pipkin, J.P. Page 455.

John F. Fortner and Prudence Guice, 9 Jan. 1859, by Oats S. Lewis, J.P. Page 455.

Thomas W. Nolin and Hellen Mae Harrell, 30 Dec. 1858, at Priscilla Watson's, by Jack Hardman, J.P. Page 456.

William O. Moore and Mary Jane Kent, issued 1 Jan. 1859, return not recorded. Page 456.

B. F. Reaves and Henrietta Brigman, 2 Jan. 1859, at Jas. K. Turner's, by A. H. Justice, J.P. Page 457.

George W. Worthington and Lucinda E. Simms, 2 Jan. 1859, at Joel Simms', by R. E. Brown. Page 457.

E. D. Carter and Mary Ramsey, 20 Jan. 1859, by A. H. Justice, J.P. Page 457.

Zachariah Bush and Suphroney Dubose, 6 Jan. 1859, at Seborn Dubose's, by B. Williams, J.P. Page 458.

James B. Dubose and Anah H. Hodges, 11 Jan. 1859, at A. H. Hodges', by R. E. Brown. Page 458.

James H. Wise and Ann E. Stewart, issued 11 Jan. 1859, return not recorded. Page 458.

O. H. Freeman and Eliza S. Dinkins, 18 Jan. 1859, at Glennville, by Jno. Crowell, M.G. Page 459.

William H. Cunningham and Sarah Clark, 16 Jan. 1859, by R. E. Brown. Page 459.

James H. Hardrick and Elizabeth Ray, 20 Jan. 1859, at M. Ray's, by Elijah Ray, J.P. Page 459.

Benjamin N. Hendrix and Miss H. V. G. Conner, 20 Jan. 1859, by Green Malone. Page 460.

Hannibal Harper and Lurrey Stephenson, 1 Feb. 1859, at Council Stephenson's, by Wm. Ross, M.G. Page 460.

W. A. Jones and Georgiana Creal, 27 Jan. 1859, at Thos. Creal's, by D. McGilvary, J.P. Page 460.

Thomas Flournoy and Ellen M. Baker, 25 Jan. 1859, at Eufaula, by L. C. Harrison, M.G. Page 461.

Thomas Holder and Mary Girley, 27 Jan. 1859, at Mrs. Coly Girley's, by O. S. Lewis, J.P. Page 461.

S. J. S. Cawthorn and Lydia E. Pynes, 27 Jan. 1859, by D. A. Bush, J.P. Page 461.

William Sheppard and Rachel Sherry, 30 Jan. 1859, at S. K. Shery's, by Aaron Helms. Page 462.

J. H. Evans and Miss A. B. Patterson, 1 Feb. 1859, by W. M. Motly, M.G. Page 462.

Henry A. Thomas and Miss F. E. Hunt, 13 Feb. 1859, at Eufaula, by Z. J. Daniel, J.P. Page 462.

A. G. Smith and Annah E. Johnson, 10 Feb. 1859, by L. P. Golson, M.G. Page 463.

Henry Day and Ann F. Seals, 13 Feb. 1859, at John D. Seals', by G. C. Efurd. Page 463.

W. G. Spurlock and Martha A. Driskill, 10 Feb. 1859, by Elijah Ray, J.P. Page 463.

Malichi Quick and Louisa Hinson, 11 Feb. 1859, by T. A. Hightower, J.P. Page 463.

W. G. Nolin and Amelia Cook, 19 Feb. 1859, at Avery Nolin's, by A. E. Jones, J.P. Page 464.

John Candry and Caroline Turner, issued 14 Feb. 1859, return not recorded. Page 464.

John R. Burke and Julia Highsmith, issued 15 Feb. 1859, executed at Thos. H. Moody's, by S. F. Lightner. Page 464.

Richmond W. Long and Martha Heron, 16 Feb. 1859, by G. C. Efurd. Page 465.

Richard Day and Mary Garner, 24 Feb. 1859, at John Garris', by Miles McInnis, J.P. Page 465.

Burrel Philips and Caroline M. Ivy, 20 Feb. 1859, by Miles McInnis, J.P. Page 465.

Thomas B. Picket and Samantha Willis, 27 Feb. 1859, at Asa Willis', by Thomas Guice, M.G. Page 466.

Ellington Battle and Susan Bullock, 22 Feb. 1859, at James E. Palmer's, by A. E. Jones, J.P. Page 466.

Robert Tate and Nancy Bailey, 24 Feb. 1859, at W. Jas. Bailey's, by A. E. Jones, J.P. Page 467.

James B. Davis and Eliza Shanks, 8 Mar. 1859, at J. K. Turner's, by A. H. Justice, J.P. Page 467.

Henry Smith and Lucinda Padget, 14 Mar. 1859, at Lucinda Padget's, by O. S. Lewis, J.P. Page 467.

Nathan Williams and Martha Lewis, 16 Apr. 1859, at Wm. M.
        Snead's, by Wm. M. Snead, J.P. Page 468.

Alexander Johnson and Kitty F. Lott, issued 23 Feb. 1859, return
        not recorded. Page 468.

Silas Helms and Nancy Hudson, issued 23 Mar. 1859, return not
        recorded. Page 468.

Thomas Jordan and Mary Fegan, 13 Apr. 1859, at B. H. Emerson's,
        by Elder Wm. Lee. Page 469.

James Stinson and Martha Senn, 14 Apr. 1859, by J. G. McLendon,
        J.P. Page 469.

William H. Keith and Mary Ann Jones, 26 Apr. 1859, at Samuel
        Jones', by Joel Sims, J.P. Page 469.

Allen Brown and Melberry J. E. Edwards, 4 May 1859, at David
        Edwards', by J. J. Phillips, J.P. Page 469.

Andrew M. Lain and Margaret Retincey Ann Gilmore, 8 May 1859,
        at Jno. Gilmore's, by S. B. Roberts. Page 470.

Henry Conyers and Mary A. L. Foutch, issued 7 May 1859, return
        not recorded. Page 470.

T. E. Barnett and Ellen V. Glenn, 12 May 1859, at M. M. Glenn's,
        by Wm. A. McCarty. Page 470.

A. J. H. Dunn and Sarah Hammock, 12 May 1859, by D. A. Bush, J.P.
        Consent of her father, Thomas Hammock. Page 471.

Alexander Gilmore and Hester Jane Stuckey, 29 May 1859, at Owen
        Stuckey's, by C. A. Parker, M.G. Page 471.

William Blakey, Jr. and Martha Ann Hartzog, 26 May 1859, at Jas.
        Hartzog's, by E. S. Warr, J.P. Page 471.

Irvin Singletery and Francis Law, 26 May 1859, by Isaac Clayton,
        M.G.   Consent of her father, Edmond Law. Page
        472.

James M. Stanford and Sarah E. Scott, 8 June 1859, at Eufaula,
        by Jas. S. Paulin. Consent of her father, T.
        Scott. Page 472.

Obed Lee and Sarah Houston, 7 June 1859, at Edward Houston's,
        by A. E. Jones, J.P. Page 473.

John M. Bludworth and Miss H. E. Woods, 21 June 1859, at
        Eufaula, by E. McNair, M.G. Page 473.

John W. Sauls and Sanpta Ann Stewart, 10 June 1859, executed at
        Thomas Stewart's. Page 473.

J. R. Massey and Francis Wilder, 16 June 1859, at J. Wilder's,
        by Jas. A. Scarborough, J.P. Page 474.

James M. Buford and Mrs. M. C. Wallace, 14 June 1859, at Dr. Wm.
        L. Cowen's, by E. McNair, M.G. Page 474.

Moses B. Phillips and Rachael Cope, 16 June 1859, by G. J.

McMurray, J.P.   Page 474.

Lovard Lee, Sr. and Sarah Jane Polk, 26 June 1859, at Lovard
        Lee's, Jr., by Judge J. S. Williams.   Page 475.

William J. Williams and Louisa Francis Lunsford, 30 June 1859, at
        J.P. Lunsford's, by G. J. McMurray, J.P.   Page 475.

John Post and Mary E. Hooten, 5 July 1859, at J. A. Hooten's,
        by G. J. McMurray, J.P.   Page 475.

Green B. Lunsford and Clementine A. Black, 10 July 1859, by
        S. H. Dent, J.P.   Page 476.

John W. Parmer and Angelene Thomas, 14 July 1859, at Jonathan
        Thomas', by D. A. Bush, J.P.   Page 476.

William Gratehouse and Mary E. Renfroe, 10 July 1859, by G. R.
        Scroggins, J.P.   Page 476.

Green Wood and Mary Hardwick, 17 July 1859, at R. M. Hardwick's,
        by Elijah Ray, J.P.   Page 477.

John H. Barker and Lusana Mary Elizabeth Davis, 13 July 1859,
        at Epsey Davis', by G. W. Barker, M.G.   Page 477.

F. M. Pickett and Elizabeth Stovall, 28 July 1859, by J. J.
        Dickson, M.G.   Page 477.

Benjamin E. Kendrick and Mary R. Owens, 7 Aug. 1859, by E. Y.
        Van Hoose.   Page 477.

Lee Henry and Rebecca Phillips, 9 Aug. 1859, at Mrs. Ester
        Phillips', by Jas. Gary, J.P.   Page 478.

Santford Dees and Ann Gregg, issued 9 Aug. 1859, return not
        recorded.   Page 478.

William W. Searcy and Collispie C. Jones, 16 Aug. 1859, at
        Seaborn T. Jones', by Elijah Ray, J.P.   Page 479.

William E. Ventress and Mary E. Johnson, 18 Aug. 1859, at Mrs.
        Johnson's, by C. A. Parker, M.G.   Page 479.

John R. Sikes and Mary Jane Ethridge, 25 Aug. 1859, at Thos.
        Ethridge's, by Elijah Ray, J.P.   Page 479.

L. D. Spurgers and Alletha A. Wilder, 28 Aug. 1859, at John
        Wilder's, by S. B. Roberts, J.P.   Page 480.

Isaac Gratehouse and Mary E. Dawson, 24 Aug. 1859, at John
        Dawson's, by Oats S. Lewis, J.P.   Page 480.

James P. Johns and Martha J. Price, 24 Aug. 1859, by D. A. Bush,
        J.P.   Page 480.

Senchew Hunter and Sarah Ann Pool, issued 24 Aug. 1859, return
        not recorded.   Page 481.

William W. Williamson and Elizabeth M. Holmes, 9 Aug. 1859, at
        Henry Holmes', by H. H. Moreland, J.P.   Page 481.

L. A. Joiner and Miss E. G. Reynolds, 30 Aug. 1859, by R. E.

Brown, J.P. Page 481.

J. T. Johnson and Nancy A. Stephens, 5 Sept. 1859, at G. Stephens'
by Wm. B. Neal, M.G. Page 482.

W. B. Johnson and Savannah Ann Stokes, issued 3 Sept. 1859,
return not recorded. Page 482.

William Hartzog and Mary A. Horn, 8 Sept. 1859, at Nathan
Horn's, by E. S. Warr, J.P. Page 483.

Martin Cutchin and Rhoda Baxly, 15 Sept. 1859, at James Baxley's,
by E. S. Warr, J.P. Page 483.

John W. Persons and Eliza P. Pearsons, issued 6 Sept. 1859,
return not recorded. Page 483.

James L. Carrthers and Lurena Wheeler, 1 Sept. 1859, at Clayton,
by A. Van Hoose. Page 484.

Thomas Holeman and Mrs. Sarah Hughs, 11 Sept. 1859, by James
Herrod, M.G. Page 484.

Henry Oppet and Nancy Sheppard, 15 Sept. 1859, at Chas.
Sheppard's, by S. K. Shora, J.P. Page 484.

William A. Andrews and Laura E. Wilson, 21 Sept. 1859, at Levi
Wilson's, by G. Malone, M.G. Pagr 485.

Eli Justice and Mrs. Ann E. A. Justice, 25 Sept. 1859, by J. J.
Dickson, M.G. Page 485.

L. J. Ryan and Mrs. S. J. McDavid, 25 Sept. 1859, at Eli Horn's,
by H. L. Tiller, L.D. Page 485.

John B. Turner and Miss S. L. Crocker, issued 24 Sept. 1859,
return not recorded. Page 485.

Thomas J. Brown and Eliza A. Redman, 29 Sept. 1859, at Mrs.
Redman's, by Judge J. S. Williams. Page 486.

William Jones and Mrs. Nancy A. Futch, 3 Oct. 1859, by Samuel
S. Lightner, J.P. Page 486.

James R. Stinson and Emily Talbot, 5 Oct. 1859, at Henry Rains',
by S. H. Dent, J.P. Page 487.

Stephen Lunsford and Nancy Green, 13 Oct. 1859, at Wm. King's,
by Jack Hardman, J.P. Page 487.

Seaborne S. Grissett and Amanda Briger, 16 Oct. 1859, at Jno.
Newton's, by James Harrod, M.G. Page 487.

Abraham Miller and Caroline Ethredge, 16 Oct. 1859, at Thos.
Ethredge's, by Phillip Belcher, M.G. Page 488.

James W. Wilks and Nancy N. Armstrong, 27 Oct. 1859, at W. S.
Armstrong's, by Elder Wm. Lee. Page 488.

Warren W. Goolsbee and Synthia A. Evans, 1 Nov. 1859, at Mrs.
Evans, by E. Y. Van Hoose. Page 488.

John Bass and Abigail Hudson, 25 Oct. 1859, executed at N.

Hudson's. Page 489.

Levin Price and Sinthey McLeod, 24 Oct. 1859, at Clayton, by
    Joel Sims, M.G. Page 489.

W. T. Helms and Julia Ann Elizabeth Benton, 9 Nov. 1859, at J.
    Benton's, by Aaron Helms. Page 489.

N. B. Sutton and Sarah Hall, 6 Nov. 1859, at N. B. Sutton's, by
    H. H. Moreland. Page 490.

Robert S. Fillingam and Mrs. Mary E. Corbit, 2 Nov. 1859, by
    Wm. M. Snead, J.P. Consent of his mother, Mary
    Fillingam. Page 490.

John W. Johnson and Georgia Ann Williams, 9 Nov. 1859, at G. (?)
    Walker Williams', by A. E. Jones. Page 490.

Enos E. James and Antonet Emerson, 14 Nov. 1859, at Robt.
    Bevil's, by Oates S. Lewis, J.P. Page 491.

Alexander Johnson and Nancy A. S. S. Cobb, 10 Nov. 1859, at
    Mrs. Cobb's, by E. Y. Van Hoose. Page 491.

J. A. Garland and Sarah Jane Stephenson, 13 Nov. 1859, at C.
    Stephenson's, by R. E. Brown, J.P. Page 491.

Thomas Weathers and Virginia Ready, 17 Nov. 1859, at Richard
    Ready's, by S. F. Pilly, M.G. Page 492.

James Hinson and Martha D. Gannon, 20 Nov. 1859, at Wm. Gannon's,
    by Wm. M. Davis, M.G. Page 492.

Evan Brooks and Charlotte Benson, 22 Nov. 1859, at Mrs. Susannah
    Benson's, by G. J. McMurray. Page 492.

Andrew Killpatrick and Polly Roberts, 24 Nov. 1859, by Judge
    J. S. Williams. Page 493.

Thomas J. Fuller and Mary Ross, 25 Nov. 1859, by R. E. Brown,
    J.P. Page 493.

Martin E. Tyler and Piercy C. Wood, 27 Nov. 1859, at Clinton
    Wood's, by L. L. Pierce, J.P. Page 493.

Junius R. Battle and Sarah B. Hunter, 29 Nov. 1859, at Eufaula,
    by J. E. Dawson, M.G. Page 494.

Marvin Johnson and Mary Clark, 29 Nov. 1859, at Jno. Clark's,
    by R. E. Brown, J.P. Page 494.

Philip Johnson and Mary Passmore, 29 Nov. 1859, by E. S. Warr,
    J.P. Page 494.

J. B. Smith and Susan R. Hatcher, 1 Dec. 1859, at Jas. Watkins',
    by Wm. M. Snead, J.P. Page 495.

James A. Bass and Ann Dill, 13 Dec. 1859, at Clayton, by
    Augustus C. Bass, M.G. Page 495.

George W. Patterson and Margaret McIntosh, 20 Dec. 1859, at
    Daniel McIntosh's, by R. B. Brooks, M.G. Page
    496.

Sylvester Martin and Martha A. Johnson, 20 Dec. 1859, at H. G.
          Glover's, by P. M. Calloway, M.G.   Page 496.

William Ataway and Mary Cooper, issued 21 Dec. 1859, return not
          recorded.   Page 496.

William J. H. Edwards and Jane Hagler, 21 Dec. 1859, at Calhoun
          Hagler's, by J. J. Philips.   Page 497.

Henry Mooneyham and Sarah Commander, 29 Dec. 1859, at Jno.
          Commander's, by H. H. Moreland, J.P.   Page 497.

Marvin Green and Jane Lewis, 25 Dec. 1859, at Jos. Henderson's,
          by G. C. Efurd, J.P.   Page 497.

Edward Roberts and Clarisey F. Odum, 29 Dec. 1859, at James
          Odum's, by Jas. G. Tison, M.G.   Page 497.

Neill Morrison and Mary Ann Bush, 29 Dec. 1859, at Wm. Allen's,
          by D. A. Bush, J.P.   Page 498.

NAMES OF PEOPLE LISTED IN THIS BOOK; NAMES IN INDEX OF MARRIAGE
          BOOK AND PAGE NO. IN THIS BOOK

Vemtine Earnest - Volentine Earnest - Page No. 3.

Joice Eliza Shepperd - Jane E. Sheppard - Page No. 3.

Susanah Hearn - Susanah Heron - Page No. 5.

Elizabeth Amanda Ziterower - Elizabeth Amanda Ziterow - Page 5.

Rebecca Bushup - Rebecca Bishop - Page 7.

Zacharia Wesly Parmer - Zachariah Wesly Parmer - Page 8.

Cary P. Woolf and Huldale Jourdon - Cary Wolf and Hulda Jourdon
          Page 9.

Catharine Epshaw - Catharine Upshaw - Page 11.

John Warrick - John Warnick - Page 11.

Cloah Hays - Chloe Hays - Page 12.

Mary Ann Hearing - Mary Ann Herring - Page 13.

Polly Ann Reves - Polly Ann Reaves - Page 18.

Elfreda E. Rosenburg and Grbriel R. Capers - G.R. Capers to
          E. E. Rosenburg - Page 27.

Lucinda Bradberry - Given name in the index - Page 33.

Naroesa Cowan - Nancy Cowan - Page 44.

Sealy Kelly - Sarah Kelly - Page 44.

Elisha Carrol - Eliza Carroll - Page 45.

Abner A. Baleigh - A. A. Bailey - Page 47.

Caroline M. J. Ruse - C. M. J. Rouse - Page 51.

Crayton Dicken - Crayton Dickson - Page 54.

John Barber - J. Barbour - Page 59.

James B. Herain and Rachael Raburg - James B. Hearn & R. Rasburg
          Page 60.

77; James, 37; John J., 37; Lucy
A., 45; M. G., 77;
CUNNINGHAM: D., 61; Elizabeth, 24;
Flora H., 5; J. K., 52; Jane, 5;
John, 66; Josiah, 31; Margaret
R., 61; Martha, 33; Peter, 67;
William H., 98
CURENTON: Dock, 78
CURETON: Kisiah, 57; Nancy, 57;
William A., 80
CURINTON: Rhoda, 18
CURITON: Wilson, 15
CURRY: Cary, 20
CURZER: Martha M. C., 26
CUSHMAN: George S., 52; George, 36, 40
CUTCHIN: Martin, 102
DALE: Robert O., 11
DANBY: Hiram, 45
DANER: Maryan, 45
DANFORD: Daniel, 18; Edmond, 62;
Eli M., 28; James, 55; John N., 55
DANFORTH: J. H., 8, 10; Laura, 62
DANIEL: Allen, 98; Elvira M., 46;
James L., 7, 8, 10, 11, 13, 14
17, 18, 21; John, 1; Joseph, 1-3;
Joseph, Sr., 9; Juliet A., 62;
Levi L., 17; Margarett, 71;
Missouri F., 51; Moses, 1; Nancy
H., 98; Sarah E., 92; 2, J., 16,
20, 22, 25, 26, 59, 61, 63, 66,
71, 78, 84, 85, 96, 99
DANIELS: Allen, 59; John, 57
DANNER: J., 89; James W., 89;
Joseph, 89
DANSBY: Isam M., 69; Mary Jane, 69
DANSEY: Sarah, 74
DAUL: Martha, 45
DAVID: J. C., 85; W. H., 86
DAVIS: Amanda, 35; Ann H., 54; B.
F., 50; Benjamin A.,25; David, 50;
Drucilla D., 79; Elender, 88;
Eliza, 53; Epsey, 101; James B.,
99; James D, 88; James J., 70;
James M., 94; John A, 78; John
B., 92; John F., 72; John, 32, 88;
Jonathan, 33, 95; E.P.M., 97;
Lusana Mary Elizabeth, 101; Martha
Ann E., 52; Martha, 61; Mr., 79;
Rachael, 4; Sarentha A. E., 36;
Sterling, 21; Thomas H., 90;
Thomas, 49; Wm. M., 67, 90; Wm.
M., 69, 103
DAWKINS: Absolam T., 38; Alexander,
75; J. N., 72; R. H., 51
DAWSON: J. E., 103; John, 94, 101;
Joseph, 30, 94; Mary E., 101
DAY: Henry, 99; James, 49; M., 96;
Mary Ann, 63; Ransom, 63; Richard,
99; Thomas, 79; William, 15
DEAL: Ezekiel, 25
DEAN: Nancy, 96
DEAS: Isam, 65; Mack, 78
DEES: Stanford, 101
DEFFNAL: D. J. 91
DELAFIELD: Artimisia, 14
DELASHAW: John S., 65;
Drucilla Jan, 19
DELLAFIELD: Emily, 29
DELOACH: John, 97; Samuel, 40
DELONY: Frank, 83
DENSEY: Caracey Eliza, 20
DENNARD: J. S., 53, 54;
Jerrod Sanders, 39
DENNIS: Fair, 46; William, 46
DENSON: Ann H., 42
DENT: Emma, 82; J. H., 88;
John H., 68; S. H., 101, 102
DESAZO: Caroline, 11
DESHAZO: B. F., 25; Elizabeth, 10;
Georgia Ann, 29; M. W., 92;
Martha 16; Nancy, 76; Paul H., 47
DICKEN: Crayton, 54, 104
DICKENS: Burton L., 57
DICKINSON: J. J., 43; J. L., 94;
John F., 55
DICKSON: Crayton, 104; J.J., 46-48,
52-54, 59, 60, 71, 75, 76, 80, 83,
84, 67, 69, 101, 102; Susan, 58
DIKES: David, 6; Seney, 4
DILL: Ann, 103; Mary Jane, 22;
Robert, 67; Sarah D., 8; Sarah, 15
DILLARD: Edward, 86; Mary E., 86
DILLESHAW: Emily, 51; Susan, 50
DINKINS: Eliza S., 98
DIXON: J. J., 72, 86,
DIXSON: J. J., 85
DOBBS: John, 22
DOGGET: B. F., 21
DORMAN: Eliza, 48; Mary, 25;
William Ag. 83
DOSTER: O. C., 54; Thomas, 12
DOUGHTERY: Jane, 8
DOUGLAS: D. S. T., 84, 90, 94
DOWLIN: Elizabeth, 96
DOWLING: Benjamin L., 90; E.G., 32;
Elias, 86; Emaline, 28; Hansford,
25; Lena, 32; Mary A., 32; Mary,
Nancy 86; Nancy, 8, 86
DRAKE: V. G., 97; Washington F., 28
DRAPER: Martha, 2, 84; Mary Ann, 78;
Peter, 78; William, 86
DREGGARS: Charles A.,47

DREW: Manning, 54
DRIGGARS: James, 51
DRIGGERS: Stephen, 72
DRISKELL: Martha A., 99
DUBOSE: Desnabo, 6; Drucilla, 55;
E. E., 70; Eleson, 39; Isalh, 30;
James B., 98; Joel, 54; John P.,
92; Julia E., 70; Martha E.J., 42;
Mary E., 61; Middleton, 15; Nancy,
44; Peny, 62; Robert, 9; Saleann
B., 29; Seaborn J.,29; Seborn, 98;
Suphroney, 98; Susan, 6;
William J., 30
DUDLEY: George W., 69
DUFFELL: John D., 51
DUKE: Louise E., 50; Rhody Ann, 56
DUKES: Amanda J., 46; David, 66;
Elizabeth, 66; Mary S., 37;
Sarah, 53; William, 66
DUNN: A. J. H., 100; Levi, 33, 75
DURDEN: Elisha, 71; James F., 68
DYKES: Elizabeth, 7; Isaac, 36;
Martha, 7; William, 41
EARLY: Sarah, 10
EARNEST: Ventine, 3, 104;
Volentine, 104
EARP: Caleb W., 75; Flewellen, 61;
Lewella, 84; Margaret, 61;
Martha A. M., 70
EASTERLING: Daniel B., 90, 94;
David S., 44; Rebecca, 94
ECHOLS: Clark, 81; Lanyann, 81
ECHOLS: S. C., 75
ECKOLS: Elizabeth, 15
EDGE: Eli, 97; Jane, 74; Lewis, 53;
Mrs., 74; Sarah, 24
EDGLER: John, 68
EDWARDS: David, 100; G. W., 9;
Melberry J., 8, 100; P. H., 20;
William J. H., 104
EFURD: G. C., 88, 93, 95, 96, 99,
104; G. E., 98; Giles C., 59;
Louisa, 66; T. C., 2, 6, 7,
9, 10, 12, 13, 18, 24, 66; Thomas
C., 78; W. T. J. C., 81
EIDSON: Emily, 55; Mrs., 75; Nancy,
75; Owen, 17; Wiley, 33
ELDER: Wilmouth, 1
ELDRIDGE: Peter., 9
ELEY: Howell T., 9
ELKINS: Irvin, 19
ELLIS: Elizabeth, 26, 33; Joseph,
56; Julia, 8; Mary, 34; Nancy, 54;
Thomas, 60; Unity, 47; William
J., 54, 64, 67, 86
ELLISON: William H., 61, 83, 88, 97,
ELMER: John W., 20
ELMORE: Mark, 47
EMERSON: Antonet, 103; B.H., 65, 96,
100; Martha, 96; Sarah, 65
ENGLISH: Catharine, 83; George, 80;
John A., 99
EPPERSON: Amanda, 65
EPSHAW: Catharine, 11, 104
ETHREDGE: Stephen W., 84
ETHRIDGE: Caroline, 102; Thos., 102
ETRIDGE: James M., 72; John B., 46;
Mary Jane, 101; Shadrock, 91;
Thos. 101
EUBANKS: Francis, 68; Mary, 68;
Mrs., 72; Rebecca Ann, 72
EUFURD: Lucyann, 11; Rebecca L., 12
EVAN: E. M, 79
EVANS: Adeline, 63; Amelia Ann, 83;
Andrew, 67; Charles, 18, 56; 57;
Edmonel, 33; Elizabeth, 89; J.H.,
9; J.L.C., 30; Jane, 43; Mahala,
6; Mrs.,102; Sophrona, 79; Synthia
A., 102; William J., 56; William,
73, 89; Wm., 63
EVERETT: Dillan, 82; Edey, 87;
Jourdan, 82; Sherman B., 93
FAILS: Elizabeth, 31
FAISON: A. M., 99; James D., 70;
Martha, 1; Nancy, 47; Thomas J.,
38; W. D., 72-73; William, 60
FANER: Amon E., 79
FAQUA: Randall, 35
FARMER: Margarett, 57; Mary, 94;
Ottis Edgington, 1; Sarah A., 55;
William, 92
FARRAR: Harriet A., 58
FAULK: Elizabeth A., 96; Elizabeth
Ann, 16; George G.B., 60; George
W., 16; Henry S., 17; Henry, 32,
34, 42, 53, 96; Henry, J.,
1, 12, 16, 47, 19, 21, 23, 26, 27;
Henry, Jr., 34-37, 42, 45, 48,
50, 54-55, 57, 59, 61; James K.,
27; Jesse, 11; John W., 32; Julia
V., 85; Kisiah, 15; L. 76, 85;
Lorenzo, 98; Lucretia J., 76; Mark
W., 42; Martha C., 98; Mary, 76;
Nancy 86; Nancy, 8, 86
FAVORS: William R., 35
FEAGAN: Martha Ann, 2; Nancy, 59;
Samuel, 43
FEGAN: Mary, 100
FENN: J. T., 84; Lucinda, 30;
Mathew, 50, 71; Rebecca R., 71
FERGOR: John R., 22
FIELD: Henry H., 63

FILIMGAM: Sarah, 18
FILLINGAM: Mary, 103; Mellal, 27;
Robert S., 103
FILLINGHAM: Emily, 31
FILLINGIM: Eliza M, 35
FLAKE: Elinnah E., 84; Florida, 80;
Sarah J., 37; Seborn J., 6,
FLEMING: Caleb, 27; Emily F., 63;
J., 63; Oliver, 58, 64, 67, 89,
92; Robert A., 95; Theresa Ann
Elizabeth, 17
FLEMINS: Elizabeth, 47
FLEMMING: William, 45
FLETCHER: John, 22
FLEWELLEN: Antolnett V.,37; E.R., 97
FLINN: Elizabeth, 41; Esther R., 66;
John, 66
FLOID: Nancy J., 2
FLORENCE: Mr., 97; Obadiah, 18
FLOURNOY: A.S., 28; C.E., Miss, 96;
James E., 28; James, 28; L. S.,
Mrs., 32; M. V., Miss, 81; Nancy,
28; Robert, 82; S.A.M., Miss, 93;
Thomas, 99
FLOWERS: Avender, 36; Bethena, 18;
Harrell, 22; Jincy, 22; Littleton,
15; Priscello, 22; Rebecca, 63;
William, 58; Willis, 27; Wright, 69
FLOYD: Harriet L., 54; James R. J.,
78; Jeanette Margaret, 20; Joseph,
84; Mary, 75; Michael W., 73;
Mrs., 75; Poly Ann, 15;
Theophulus, 54
FORAN: Huey, 33
FORD: Antonette, 86; E.C.N., 94;
Eli N., 95; James, 4; W. G., 86
FOREHAND: Henry, 95; John, 90;
Nancy, 68; Stephen, 68, 90, 92
FORT: Elizabeth, 40; William H., 44
FORTE: J. A., Miss, 42
FORTNER: Emeliza, 84; John F., 98
FORTSON: Lucy A., 58; T. W., 58
FOSEY: J. J.
FOSTER: J. L., 94; John M., 19;
Thomas H., 30, 31
FOUTCH: Mary A. L., 100
FOWLER: Narcessy L., 95; Susan M.,80
FRANKLIN: Rebecca, 85; T., 85
FRASER: Malcom, 3; W. T., Miss, 67
FRASIER: Ebenezer, 21
FREEMAN: Mary, 25; O.H., 98; Sarah
A., 74; William, 74
FRY: Adaline, 91; Elizabeth, 26
FRYER: Rachel Ann, 84; Richard H.,30
FULLER: Thomas J., 103
FULTON: John, 25
FUQUA: Elizabeth, 44; Elizabeth,
78; Sterling, 78
FURMAN: William, Jr., 70
FUTCH: Nancy A., Mrs., 102
GACHET: Annie, 83; Charles B., 89
GACHETT: Adelade C., 89
GALLAWAY: George W., 73; John W., 20
GALLOWAY: J. W., 13, 45, 47-49, 53
GAMMAN: Sarah E., 93
GANN: Margaret, 93
GANNON: Daniel M.,97; Martha D.,103
GANNON: Wm., 103
GARDNER: Ann, 28; Benjamin, 31;
Colin, 39
GARLAND: Adalan, 82; E.J., Miss, 86;
J. A., 103; L. A., Miss, 85;
Washington, 82
GARNER: Mary, 99
GARRETT: Elizabeth, 17
GARRIS: John, 16, 99
GARVIN: Louise L., 46
GARY: James, 55, 60, 61, 63, 72, 76,
77, 79, 80, 82, 84, 91, 95, 101;
William L., 24
GASTON: A. L., 59
GAUGHT: Rebecca, 4
GAY: J. L., 22
GERKEY: F. M., Miss, 81
GIBBINS: Savanah J., 78
GIBONS: L., 72
GIBSON: Joseph D., 9; Julia Ann,
80; Nancy, 24; Sarah E., 78;
William H. C., 93
GIDDING: Isaac, 30
GIDDINGS: Eley Ann, 51; Eliza J.,
59; Mitchel, 34
GILBERT: John B., 56
GILCHRIST: Caroline G.,85; Catherine,
40; Daniel, 28; M., 40, 49, 53-55,
58, 61, 62; Malcom, 25, 46, 48,
51; Mr., 71; Nancy M., 71
GILES: Henry, 46
GILFORD: John A., 31
GILLINWATER: James A.,42; John W.,77
GILLIS: Christian, 66; D.,19; Daniel
H., 34; Donald, 6, 12; Hugh, 44;
Hughey, 56; John, 2; John, Jr.,
85; Murdock, 3; Neel, 28
GILLMORE: Jacob, 89
GILMER: Levina, 9
GILMORE: Alexander, 100; Eli, 11;
George Washington, 97; Jno., 100;
Margaret A., 91; Margaret
Retincey Ann, 100
GINNRIGHTS: Sarah, 47
GINWRIGHT: Martha A., 83;

Nancy, 48; Reesey, 21
HUTTO: Allen, 45; Elizabeth, 7;
  Henry J.,
HUTTSON: Dicy, 8
HYAT: Julia, 22
INGRAM: John F., 61; Mary J., 75;
  O. C., 75
IRVIN: James A. B., 95
IRWIN: Samuel D., 46
IVINSON: Martha, 56
IVY: Alsey A., 34; Caroline M., 99;
  John T.,77; Joseph, 77; Josephine,
  53; Nancy Jane, 73; Robert, 33;
  William, 20
JACKSON: Candis, 10; Charles J.,
  53; Drucilla, 16; Francis H., 17;
  Gillis, 45; James, 3; Julian, 3;
  Margaret A., 53; Mary, 8, 51;
  Robert N. 1; Warren D., 83;
  William H., 23; William A.,
JACOBS: Allen, 61
JAMES: Daniel D., 60; Edwin, 9, 22,
  30, 33, 37, 39, 41, 42,46, 47, 56,
  57, 59, 60, 62, 67, 68,; Enos E.,
  103; Harriet E. 56; James B., 57;
  John B., 76; John P., 37;
  Sarah E., 57
JAMISON: Jesse, 19
JARRELL: Willis S., 20
JARRETT: Mary Ann, 52
JEFFCOAT: Adaline, 81; Eliza, 81;
  Franklin, 81
JEMISON: John, 29
JENKINS: Caroline Harvey, 18;
  Elisha, 83; Isham, 96; Nancy, 93
JENNINGS: M. H., Miss,57
JERNIGAN: Frances A.,43; William, 16
JERRY: Delilla, 51
JOCHNSON: Felder, 8
JOHN: Francis, 8
JOHNS: Francis, 76; James P., 101
JOHNSON: A.J., 52; Alexander, 100,
  103; Alexr. M.,47; Andrew P., 94;
  Annah E., 99; Axey, 75; Caroline,
  56; Charity, 28; David W. 97;
  David, 29, 90; Elizabeth E., 27;
  Emanuel, 69; Frances, 28; J.D.,
  69; J.E. 88 J.H. 102; James
  B., 20, 23; James D., 52; James
  S., 20; James, 7; John M., 65;
  John W., 103; John, 23; L.A.T.,
  82; Louisa A., 91; Lusinda, 12;
JOHNSON: Mariana, 18; Marjery, 73;
  Martha A., 75, 104; Martha J., 42;
  Martha, 21, 92; Marvin, 103; Mary
  A., 34; Mary E., 101; Mary J., 86;
  Mary, 11; Mrs., 91, 101; Nancy
  Ann, 82; Patience, 44; Philip, 92,
  103; R., 89; Samuel, 77; Sarah A.
  M.,28; Sarah, 54, 83; Thomas, 43;
  Turner, 61; W.B., 102; W.S., 64;
  William G., 89
JOHNSTON: James B., 18; James S.
  91; James, 24; Jesse F., 91; John
  W., 14; L. J. 40; Lawson, 31;
  Sarah, 45; Susan Jane, 31
JOINER: L. A., 101; Marinah, 42;
  Mary Ann, 25; Peter, 87
JONES: A. E., 60, 63-65, 67, 69,
  74-76, 79, 83, 86, 89-90, 92, 97,
  99-100, 103; Aicial, 5; Aretus
  W., 28; Catherine, 21; Charnoch,
  14; Collisple C., 101; David B., 86;
  Eliza, 5; Elizabeth, 2, 17; Emily,
  3; Genevaln S., 59; George C.,
  24; George Pitman, 94; J. A., 41,
  45; J. P., 43; James, 13, 64;
  John A., 80; John, 9; Lewis A.,
  48; Louisa, 66; Lucinda, 95;
  Margarett A., 64; Martha A., 29;
  Jones: Mary Ann, 100; Mary, 37, 40;
  Mathew, 43; Mr.,65; Perry H., 39;
  Robert N., 1; Russel, 20; Samuel,
  100; Sarah L., 10; Seaborn T.,
  101; Seaborn, 71, 73, 79, 82, 84,
  87, 90; Susan, 14; W. A., 98; V.
  R., 16; William H., 14; William
  K., 11-13, 18, 19; William R.,
  16; William, 102
JORDAN: J.W., 69; John, 53; Junius,
  94; Malisa A., 34; Mary F., 49;
  Thomas, 100; William C., 79
JORDEN: Eli, 85
JOSEY: J. J., 72
JOURDAN: Geraldine, 30; H. L., 19;
  Isham, 9; Nancy, 33
JOURDEN: Nancy, 9
JOURDON: Hulda, 104; Huldale, 9
JUSTICE: A. H., 81, 85-87, 89, 90,
  92, 95, 97-99; Ann E. A., 102;
  Edward, 60; Eli, 102; Sarah, 89
KAIGLER: M. A., Miss, 93; Reubin,
  92; Sarah C., 92
KARKLIN: Snoden, 10
KEACHEY: George, 96
KEAHEY: Elijah J., 2
KEEN: Martha D., 24
KEENER: John F., 1; Martha, 3;
  Mary, 31
KEITH: Robert, 87; William H., 100
KEIT: Adrianna C., 57
KELLY: C.J.S., 2; F.W., 74; John,

47, 56; Matilda, 15; Meranda, 22;
  Sarah, 104; Sealy, 44, 104;
  William P., 32; William, 29, 44
KEMP: Candis, 71; Caroline, 16;
  Elizabeth, 18; Thomas, 70
KENADY: Harriet, 24; William R., 28
KENDRICK: Benjamin E., 101;
  Thomas C., 2
KENEDY: Donald, 12; Joseph T., 85
KENNEDY: W. L., 89
KENNEDY: Albert S., 86; David, 47;
  John D., 96; Mary, 89
KENT: Aaron, 87; Avery, 64; Eliza
  Ann, 87; Gilford, 41, 88; Guilford,
  30; Mary Jane, 98; Mary, 64
KERKLAND: Milly, 10
KETCHAM: Mary, 52
KETCHAMP: Sarah A., 31
KEY: Eliza, 69; Emily Eliza, 69;
  Henry, 26; Thomas, 69
KIDD: James A., 10
KIELS: Albert D., 9; Elias M., 31;
  Mary E. 38, 41
KIEZER: B. H. 86
KILLINGWORTH: Sealy, 28
KILLPATRICK: Andrew, 103; J. S.,
  89; Warry, 82
KILPATRICK: Easler, 75; Harriet,
  95; Isaac D., 24; Jesse, 54;
  Laurey, 30; Mary, 67; Spicy P.,
  29; W. H., 95; William R., 20
KINARD: William D., 50
KINCHEN: Margarett D., 68; Mr., 68
KING: Abi, 89; Abner B.,2; Gabrul
  N., 73; Hiram, 7; Hybert, 17; John
  F., 80; John W., 59; Levi, 71;
  Levy, 71; Margarett, 75; P.A.T.
  Miss, 91; Rebecca J., 71; Reubin,
  29; Samuel, 73; Sarah A. D., 68;
  Sarah Ann, 80; Sarah, 64; Sheppard
  W., 86; Susan A., 71; Tandy W., 66;
  Theophilus C.,31; Thomas, 75, 80;
  W., 64; William, 42; Wm., 102
KINIMS: Mary, 38
KITCHAM: Elizabeth, 74; Mrs., 74
KNIGHT: Nathaniel, 8; Richard, 65
KUSER: B. H. 80, 82,
LAIN: Andrew M., 100
LAMAR: John O., 52; Lucy Catherine,
  7; Sallie E., 88; Thomas S., 81;
  William M., 25
LAMBERT: W. 66
LAMKIN: William M., 88
LAMPLEY: Hanah M., 46; Jacob, 65;
  John M., 27; Jonathan R., 18
LANDRUM: Pauline, 14
LANDY: Elizabeth P., 67; Elizar, 12
LANG: William H. 90
LANGFORD: Frances 58; Sarah J., 52
LANGSTON: R. G. 35
LANGSTON: William A. J., 60
LANY: John R., 47
LARDWICK: Alford H., 83
LARKINS: Elenzar, 44
LASSETER: Mathew M., 29; Mathew, 29;
  Sarah A. 57
LASITER: James R., 50; Mathew, 89
LASSETER: Martha, 52
LATEN: Alfred, 72
LATER: William, 55
LAW: Edmond, 100; Francis, 100;
  Jas., 58; John, 84; Josiah S.,
  41; Josiah, 58; Samuel L., 40, 58
LAWHORN: Henry, 71; Sarah A., 69;
  Susan Ann, 76; W. J. 71
LAWLESS: Johnson, 55; Sintha, 45
LAWRENCE: Elizabeth Jane, 17
LAWSON: W.A. B., 65
LECOUNT: John, 70
LEDBETTER: Elizabeth A., 53
LEE: David C., 6; Eliza, 23; Epsey,
  2; Godfrey, 45; Harvey, 61; J.
  C., 94; James P., 80; Jane, 96;
  Lovard, 9, 91; Lovard, Jr., 101;
  Lovard, Sr., 101; Luvina, 83;
  Martha A., 72; Mary E., 68; Mary,
  101 Mrs., 72, 90, 96; N., 68;
  Needham, 12; Needham, Sr 44;
  Noel R, 27; Obed, 100; Robert, 8;
  Sarah A., 90; Sarah, 43; Timothy
  20; W. B. W., 91; William, 25, 48,
  96; William, Elder, 38, 52, 65, 71,
  73-74, 86, 89, 91-92, 96, 100, 102
LESTER: William P., 69
LEVERETT: Mathew A., 64
LEWIS: Benjamin G., 74; Daniel G.,
  11; David, 10; Eady, Mrs., 25;
  Elias, 8, 95; Eliza, 4; Elizabeth,
  2, 51; Elmyra 1, 25; Harret, 47;
  Isac R.W., 43; Jackson, 26; James
  A., 52; Jane G., 66; Jane, 104;
  John W., 87; John, 42, 79; Mahala,
  20; Manahy, 28; Martha, 100; Mary,
  34; Milly, Mrs, 26; Nancy E., 47;
  Oats S., 81, 92, 93, 96, 98, 99,
  101 103; Sarah An, 26; Seaborn,
  2; Stephen B., 88; Z. M. L., 74
LIGGET: Thomas, 93
LIGHTNER: John M., 12; M., 62;
  Michael, 62; S.E.,93, 99; Samuel
  J., 72; Thomas S., 17, 102
LILLY: Edmund, 74

LINDSEY: Hany A., 49; Hiram F., 36;
  Jeptha, 22, 65, 70; Joseph, 90;
  Lewis, 41; Ludy Ann, 65; Nathan
  H., 70; Sempson, 20
LINGO: R. T., 77; Richard B., 77
LIPTROT: William A., 85
LITTLE: Anna C., 79; J., 79, 88;
  James P., 88; Jemima, 88; Josiah,
  89; Sarah Ann, 89
LITTLEFIELD: Henry E., 61; John, 61
LOCHALA: Katherine, 24;
  Thomas, 89, 92, 95
LOCK: Thomas S., 27
LOCKE: William B., 77
LOFLIN: Thomas, 24, 92; William, 21
LOLLESS: Nancy, 35
LOMAR: W. G., 61
LOMAX: Tennent, 35
LONG: C. P., 46; Clarkey Adeline,
  26; Comedore P., 95; Elizabeth
  L., 54; F. E. Miss, 98; Margarett
  A., 77; Micajah, 23; N. W., 98;
  Richmond W., 99; William, 55
LORE: David, 22
LOTT: Adalald, 87; Artemasia, 72;
  Arthur, 1, 22, 72, 75-76; E. G.,
  46; E. T. H. Miss, 77; Easley, 45;
  John D., 83; Kitty F., 100; Mrs.,
  87; Nancy, 78; Narcissa, 75
LOVELESS: B.D., 47, 51, 58, 67, 72,
  74, 77-78, 81-86; Benjamin D., 24;
  Jane, 14; Mary M., 24; Nancy, 65;
  Sarah, 67; Sophornia, 43; Susan
  William, 42
LOVETT: Sarah Ann, 19
LOWE: Jane M., 90; Jas. P., 40, 58;
  R. M., 86; R. N, 61, 62, 68, 72,
  73, 84, 89-90, 97
LOWMAN: Eliza C., 48; G. W., 24;
  James L., 66; John E., 16; John
  J., 77; Martha E., 66; Mrs., 66;
  S.A.E. Miss, 97; Sarah A., 16;
  Wm., 97
LUDLUM: Larkey, 20; Mary A. E., 93
LUKER: William, 38
LUNCEFORD: J. P., 85;
  Mary Jane Unity, 85
LUNSFORD: B. S., 88; Franklin B.,
  56; George W., 27; Green B., 101;
  J. P., 101; James P., 34; Jas.,
  52; Louisa Francis, 101; Stephen,
  102; Susan, 57; William T., 57
LYNCH: Thomas, 13
MABREY: James W., 76
MABURY: Joshua, 5
MADDOX: Amanda, 46
MAGRUDER: Susan, 21
MALLARD: James H., 68
MALLORY: C. A., 99
MALLROY: C. A. Miss, 60
MALONE: G. 2, 20, 55, 60, 69, 102;
  Green, 30, 47, 94, 97, 98
MALOY: Duncan, 68; Martha, 68
MANDLEY: John, 14
MANN: Emily, 9; Manning H., 11;
  Maria T., 11; Melinda A., 58;
  William B., 2, 4, 6, 10, 11,
MARCUS: Micjah, 63
MARKEY: Elizabeth Jane, 95; H. J.,
  95; James T., 32
MARLOR: Elizabeth, 64
MARLY: S. C., 66
MARSHALL: A. M., 87; Caroline, 91;
  Daniel M., 77; Sarah E., 65; T.,
  65; Thomas P., 34; Thomas, 77
MARTIN: A. J., 51; Amanda M., 48;
  C. A. E. Miss, 92; Catherine, 62;
  D. A.; Elizabeth, 54, 78; Elvira
  D., 45, 62; Emeline, 52; Floyd,
  86; George, 54; Jane, 13, 92;
  Jeremiah, 98; John Calvin, 30;
  John F., 54; John T., 18; John
  W., 46; Lucilla, 45; Lucitta, 12;
  Lydia Ann E., 88; Mrs., 75, 89;
  Nancy A. K., 48; Nancy An, 15;
  Penelope A., 89; Robert, 76; Sarah
  E., 31; Sarah, 75, 92; Sylvester,
  25, 76, 104; Thomas W.,81; Warren,
  2; William J., 79
MASSA: Lucinda, 72; Semion, 72
MASSEY: J. R., 100; John B., 75
MATHEW: W., 46;
MATHEWS: Eveline, 59; James, 15;
  M.; Mary, 80; Moses, 75
MATHISON: Malcom, 49
MAXWELL: Ruth M. M. A. J., 67
MAYNER: Mary Ann, 84
MAYO: M. D. L., 44; Telitha, 79;
  Wesley T., 44
MAYS: Samuel E., 90
MCALISTER: John W., 22
MCALLISTER: A. V., 35; John W., 28;
  Mary, 33
MCANDREWS: William A., 53
MCAPLIN: F. A., 62
MCBETH: A. W., 9
MCBRIDE: Eliza A. E., 94; Mary A.,
  60; Samuel, 47; Sarah Caroline,
  61; William J., 80
MCCALL: Daniel,58; Duncan, 55;
  Gilbert, 23; Hugh, 83; Jincy, 3;